The Glacial Stairway

PETER RILEY was born in 1940 near Manchester. He studied at Pembroke College, Cambridge, and the universities of Keele and Sussex. He has taught at the University of Odense (Denmark) and since 1975 has lived as a free-lance writer and poetry bookseller, from which he retired in 2008. He lived in the Peak District for ten years and now lives in Cambridge, with regular excursions to Transylvania, in the music and society of which he has taken a special interest.

Also by Peter Riley from Carcanet Press

Alstonefield: a poem
Passing Measures

PETER RILEY

The Glacial Stairway

CARCANET

Acknowledgements

Grateful acknowledgement is due to the editors and publishers of the following booklets and periodicals where parts of this book first appeared, some in earlier versions.

'The Glacial Stairway', Part One: *PN Review*; Part Two: *fragmente*
'Aria with Small Lights': West House Books 2003
'Best at Night Alone' (version of 23 April 2008): Oystercatcher Press 2008
'The Twelve Moons': Oystercatcher Press 2009
'Western States (2)': *Free Poetry* (Boise, Idaho) 2009

And other poems in *Axolotl*, *Broadsheet*, *Cambridge Literary Review*, *Free Verse* (website), *Half Circle*, *Horizon* (website), *Origin* (website), *PN Review*, *Shearsman*, *Tears in the Fence* and *Tenth Muse*.

First published in Great Britain in 2011 by
Carcanet Press Limited
Alliance House
Cross Street
Manchester M2 7AQ

Copyright © Peter Riley 2011

A CIP catalogue record for this book is available from the British Library

ISBN 978 1 84777 079 0

The publisher acknowledges financial assistance from Arts Council England

Supported by
**ARTS COUNCIL
ENGLAND**

Typeset by XL Publishing Services, Tiverton
Printed and bound in England by SRP Ltd, Exeter

Contents

1

2

3

The Glacial Stairway

In the summer of 1956 John Stanley, the art master of Stockport Grammar School, led a group of boys, including myself, then aged 15, over a mountain pass in the Pyrenees, from Tarascon-sur-Ariège in France into Andorra, by a little used route which he had somehow discovered. The distance walked was about fifty kilometres horizontally and one kilometre vertically. The vertical part was done in one hard day-long slog near the beginning, to get over the pass known as Port de Siguet and into Andorra. It was the first time I had ever left Britain. In June 2004 we repeated as much of this walk as we could manage, given more difficult weather conditions with a lot of snow still lying on the upper slopes, and streams which had to be crossed badly swollen by meltwater. Partly by subterfuge, we did gain the upper slopes on the Andorran side and I was again descending the great valley through El Serrat, Llorts, Ordino, to Andorra la Vella, places well remembered but changed in the intervening 48 years in ways that echoed from the entire Western world.

—oOo—

Part One

This is me 48 years ago, this is 48 of my years, the same valley
the same sky's water crashing down the gully the same
striving uphill, taking the strain, bearing the weight.
48 years, something happened in the world, what was it?
Intentions conjoined and dispersed, soldiers died.

Then I was young and in company, now we tread the steep paths together,
two experiences conjoined. And we note as we did not then
the flowers all around and the valley full of the sound of falling water,
the closing hopes as the air opens before us. We form from this air
the names that stand behind us: birds, flowers, insects, villages,
everything we know, and the dead of seven wars.

To walk with thought in the very muscle, of answering, thought of
Un mundo mejor es posible, taking the strain of disappointment by the
[thrush's
peal of pain in the dark wood. From which we emerge into the open valley
and thought of a possible speech, one that must be true, and open, and must
do good, where good can be done, and where's that? So rarely here.
Clear river shooting over stones, where is our power zone?

All of the present and all of the past, goodbye. Ahead of us
our strength is trailing away. My eyes hurt, and legs and back,
and the news places a sciatica across my frontal dream, a burning thing,
a mask. We look up to the conciling seeds, the invisible day stars
as the ground plunders our energy and the path vanishes into a stream.

Vanish with it into 48 years, excavate the air for signs of hope.
There are such: the behaviour of a beetle, the communal will
when it is free to breathe. Grass, stones, help me will you – think!
What's the answer, what are we going to do with the world?
We're going to forget it. And it us.

Had I brain and courage, I would chuck all this poetry into the skip
wouldn't you? If you thought you could actually do something to the good
that would last. Beauty may last, that stands in the space between
stone and hawk, sheer persistence on the painful routes,
where the land turns thought into its own substance, of rock,
of rhododendron bushes, of pouring water, of heart beats.
And the turning dance on each step, of modernity, the search
for inhabitable centres.

Guided by the mountain's shadow, the rock planes, the lines
of the hibiscus leaf, sight breathes a defiant longing for peace at large
in the emblem of two linked arms, spray driven off waterfalls pencil thin
on the far slope as the leaves wave from side to side and the wounds
do the couple dance, sharing their blood. The defiance and the love
bleeding into each other, over a dark stone.

A neglected track over the mountains from Ariège to Andorra by Port de
Siguer. Muleteers' route, smugglers' route, escape route for Cathars fleeing
the Inquisition, and for Jews and Resistance during the Occupation.
Merchant caravans, wide-ranging professional shepherds with flocks of
thousands, seasonal labour from the French villages to the mines and forges
at Llorts and Ordino, summer wood-gathering in the high Andorran valleys
I have trodden these paths, special goods to and from the al-Andalus courts,
manuscripts in astronomy and music, slaves, dancing girls bringing treatises
of ecstasis to militarist citadels and kick-starting European poetry *I have not
trodden alone*, bread daily in season from Tarascon and Siguer because of
Andorra's lack of cereals. Bread and Troubadors. Also a minor variant of the
pilgrimage route to Compostella. All these high passes considered dangerous
and only used late spring to early autumn *and I have now trodden twice*.

Some place in these mountains made Baudelaire think we are innately
[virtuous, at first.
'…en parfaite paix avec moi-même et avec l'universe je crois même que,
dans ma parfaite béatitude et dans mon total oubli de tout le mal terrestre,
j'en étais venu à ne plus trouver si ridicules les journaux qui prétendent
que l'homme est né bon [*hiatus*] et un morceau de gâteau… suffit
pour engendrer une guerre.' You could step into the hiatus and break your leg.

Far below us are cave systems where people have inscribed the meaning
of death many times over, how it gathers us up among our objects
into the dream funnel, the last focus, every hope and every gain
converging on the sides of the vault. That route is with us up here,
we feel it through the soles of our boots from far under, patience
and persistence, further and further from anywhere until
you meet the earth, and cast your being out from your hand
onto the wall, the closure, the surface, where it hovers and howls.

Stones and gravel underfoot to the bright music of streams
taking human weight on the turning heel. Who is this elderly gent
struggling up a Pyrenean valley, how many more years
has he got of draining strength not 48 for sure. *Who are you?*
And the bright water turns round the granite base as it will and it will.

Je suis le veilleur du Pont-au-Change, I am the watchman
of the stone bridge in the heart of the city I hear the enemy
creeping through the streets at night uttering the words of a binding
that I can't untie an enclosure I can't break. I am trying to cross
a swollen stream in the Pyrenees by leaping from clod to clod
wrapped in the surround, wrapped in privilege, daring to hope
for victims of power by trust in human resource under limitation
tears flying over the stream, curses mobilised into the sky *Je suis
le veilleur du Point de Jour.*

Water banks above glacial step. Fear and sorrow, creeping
towards the death void, the death ignorance. Loneliness, failure,
inadequacy. The world destroying all the work we've done.
The music stilled, the music wrecked, the company dispersed.
Ibn Arabi turns his back and heads for Anatolia.
Alienation from reality, disappointment, voicelessness:
unmediated, unmitigated, and largely unmeditated.
Considerable possibilities for expansion in this section.
Luchar contra lo imposible y vencer!

Overworked muscles, mounting the stairs determined beyond
any possible doubt. A good is possible. I am entitled to make elisions
between geological and moral structures. The good is where the bond serves,
between thee and me, wealth and labour, care and desire. Denying voices
in the wind, accusative hungers grasping at collective advantage.
Perhaps they are right, perhaps the world is a pit of gains.
Violets, anemones, and narcissi living in small enclaves. It's terrible
what happens to people's brains. Blame and hatred by category,
confirmation of own safety and progress by hurt and halt to other.
Water banks above glacial step to a curved lake
with floating reed beds, the mountains dip their feet in.

On up, tired, lacking sociality, forgetting how they sing together a common
melancholy, harmonies not easily replicated in modernity. Forgetting
how they warn against these heroic ventures. *Fair knight setting
out to war, cowboy angel, what will you do so far from home?* Bèth chivalièr
qui partitz tà la guèrra, T'on vatz enquèra Tan luenhe d'acì? Non vedetz
[pas que
la neuit ei pregonda, E que lo monde N'ei que chepic? don't you know,
that the night is deep, and the world a load of pain. Thus they sing
in small bars far behind us. And in palaces of contradiction they construct
thrones of difference. But difference is only one of two things.
Pick the little leaf and whistle.

The water runs down the hillsides and strolls among stones and grass,
dropping into the stream. So easily down, like a market-led culture
down into nothing, nobody interested, nothing matters, let it all fall.
Uphill struggles are for the pre-defeated. That's us, you and me,
we shall be eagles and crows.

Agents of war also trod this track, and their blind servants. Alpenroses
thick among pale scree and boulders, with their bloody flowers.
We used to live in a land but it was denied. We live
where the crow chokes and the world has gone wrong and betrayed us.
So shout at it: Sun! Sun! where are you? Come out and shine
on those who have nothing to eat. It's your duty, it's your job,
come and shine on the betrayed. *Nesci nesci suli suli, ppe la luna
e ppe li stiddi, ppe le povari picciriddi ca non d'annu di mangiari*
for the moon and the stars and the poor little ones with nothing to eat,
children of war, masses of anemones and valerian and stars concealed in light.

Which war? In 1943 they never got this far, they were stopped at Siguer
and shot against a wall (there is a plaque) *Mamma, la luna come gura
e camina trapassa i monti lu mare e la marina* And the moon turns
and travels over the sea and the mountains like a hawk
singing, I shan't change, though the rock breaks and the earth changes I
shan't. Though reduced to dust and clay and the brown leaf turns to
ash in my hand, I shan't quit this body *ti 'vo e' tton affino 'utt'òrion soma.*
And George W. Bush will not mould my soul nor uglify my poetry.

———————

At night the stars occupy their river, blazed along the skystrip,
stars pulsing like babies' mouths in the night like something calling
and calling. What does it want? Desires and thoughts mate
in the darkness around us, shadows of the things we live by
moving among the dark bushes, creating new terms while
the beautiful replete stars throb over the grey mountains
and ceaseless streams, guarding our clear eyes, that see through
the darkness beyond the shapes of night to the world's progress,
tomorrow's necessary demand.

Sitting on yellow plastic outside the tent. A night creature coughs
and heaven marshals itself over the peaks, over and above their snow streaks.
Beyond the mountains the usurpers' fingers reach to the edge
of the culture zone. On distant plains armies clash in the night,
and not a single one of them represents or in any way defends,
the human reality. On this we sleep, amid a continuous crashing.

And in the morning on and up, the final stretch
to the summit, Port de Siguer, a slight dip in a high ridge.
The planet turning, water spilling on stone, the earth
'suspended in its canticle', gathering a circuitry of light around the victims,
exalting the humble which is a thought, to stuff in the rucksack,
a thought to carry up the mountain packed between the toothbrush
and the tablets. On the paths of love and war the poor heart hesitates,
beating double, begging the earth to relent. And the prince of all my pals
is the goodwilled citizen who doesn't count.

Steady work, like carrying a child on your back in a sling, coming up
to another glacial step, a mass of pale stone blocking the valley.
There are ways up it, and streams coming down it. Age carries youth.
The child remembers: Look, father, this was where we camped in 1956!
Above the third step, grassy humps on the edge of a mountain lake.
Where is that goodness we were seeking? Is it in the height and the labour,
does it trickle out and back down to the town, is it like a clear water arriving
in people's homes? Or is it more like a living creature and if you
raise your thumb on the long road will it give you a lift? Is it an agreement?
not to take advantage of poverty, and not to jump the death queue.
We'll stop here for a while and refresh ourselves for the final strike,
it's beautiful here, a fine place to be, good. Youth carries age.

No one has ever lived here. The lake fills the valley floor,
early morning darkness lies under the eastern flanks, first sunlight
picks out raised knolls and brightens all the western slope,
that the water comes to touch. It looks as if there is no possible way
but a narrow path skirts the water's edge and will take us over rock piles
and scree slopes along the side, round the corner, out at the feeder.
Often it seems there is no possible way. Into the top valley. Every
defeated move is a step forward, a message passed on.

Up here the river divides into three or four and drapes itself across
the valley base, rattling on stones. From all sides
a constant rustling of water in motion, like thought
forming in the throat from an inner event conditioned by knowledge
and 'riddled with the sensible' and that could be a form of love
or the only form. The not-yet programmed voice, the clearing.

Up here the river divides and rattles through spaces. A sky of small clouds
moves over, a fresh wind comes down the valley in the morning.
The river to be crossed, three times, wading on the stones, the path mounting
the fellside towards the col and fading away among boulders. Stop and
                                                      [look back.

This is Nowhere, where No Name lives, in all the weathers of altitude.
A private person intrudes here, awkwardly attempting
to dry socks on a boulder in the sun. Slipping and falling against a rock,
cutting a lip open. So bright so deep the red show, like the flowers
of the alpenrose bushes all over the hillside among the pale scree
and shattered rocks an announcement of vulnerability,
A wreath to wear, of common fate, you blood red roses.

Umbrella and walking stick, rucksack and tent. Bags under the eyes.
Muttering under breath, I can't go on. Soaked ground between granite
[boulders,
and snow banks ahead. Looks like time to stop. World, wherever you are,
it is time to stop. I know you won't stop. Reaching a far point towards
[the summit
beyond which you cannot go, like the far depths of an underground river
[system,
a rock shelter, the pilgrim's goal, a logical conclusion
at which the accusers walk out of the meeting, a show of result.
A small office in the suburbs, a seat in a quiet library. Stop there,
and think, and watch the forms of earth clenching into images,
forming a crust of language at the surface of experience, where virtue coheres,
the threshold, of death as of act. And eat Alpen bars and drink melted snow.

The violins of the wind praise our slowness in double stopping, our equality
of exhaustion, the flashing, equitable whiteness of our teeth
and the red rose within them. Fruit of slow growth.
'I saw a man writing on his bones.'

48 years. It's good when things don't change too much. The world is a
[false place.
There are other places. A mountain valley crammed with knowables, a
[library of them,
descending back down towards the shops and factories out of sight.
Can we bear its knowledge on with us, can we work on the earth's table?
The parts of the world are truer than the whole. There are other wholes,
and up above everything the dancing slippers shine silver
over the grey folds of earth. And one day to join that dance
at the incorruptible bound. Forwards and upwards to life in the crystal blocks!

Descending now on south-facing slopes, the warmth drawing soil minerals
up into flower heads, that nod and flutter. Anemones, narcissus, a few
wild tulips mostly not out yet, yellow streaks on the ends of green stalks.
Desire in attendance to eyes, and up where it's cooler, gentians,
blue gentians in the grass of ridges. *Let me guide myself with*
the blue, forked torch of this flower down the darker and darker stairs
*towards Persephone's throne, who is but a voice and a darkness invisib*le.
And the small dog-violet in its vast home enters into no competition,
barks at no one, its democracy is pluralist. Nodding in the breeze
it grows like words out of lumps of sensibility, signalling consent.
Couldn't we stay up here, in the precise economy of need,
do we have to go down there into all that wastage?

Wandering among the upper slopes song-struck, coming
to a refuge, a stone hut on a shelf, looking out over
shadowy masses from a flowery mead, a glacial step.
Wash hands, curved grass under the stream, lands we never claimed.
Inside the hut a smouldering fire, a first aid kit, a broken axe.

To know from the sweetness of the news Ab la dolchor del temps novel
as the grass shakes in the wind sitting on a rock outside the hut
listening to the streams and reckoning what we have:
la boch' e-ls olhs e-l cor e-l sen – mouth, eyes, heart, mind.
A first aid kit, a broken axe, and a smouldering fire. Which is plenty.
For I shall not change, my wish is singular,
Ades es us e no-s muda is one and shall not change.
Walk downstairs and answer that voice in the night.

Nurse and feed this wish like a falcon which shall one day be set free
and fly over the currents of forward desire, and call to the comrades and
swoop down to the cut. Call this falcon 'Learning' be it no more than
a street-corner meeting after the bar's closed – but in public, in the open,
not hiding behind language weaving threats. Say as things are,
open the hut door and set the bird free, that pecks the private self.
It is difficult for a man to save himself from cobwebs in the heart.
de tela al corc'om no-s pot defendre, and claims on the world.

Now the inverted flower shines among sharp cliffs and hills.
Still hanging round the 2300m contour, reluctant to descend,
passing by snow-bestrewn lake basins, looking up at cirques,
all the waste lurking behind the ridge. A fake country,
cut-price nation, feeding off the corruption of its neighbours,
entire towns of shopping malls, the high hills wrecked by ski resorts,
the valleys thick with apartment blocks that no one lives in,
tax evasion addresses for the rich, the poor suffering old rich
who worry themselves to death. A 'fiscal paradise' called Andorra.
Just out of sight of this heaven, pausing at snow, testing its crust, sitting
uncomfortably on tufts of wiry grass by the lake with cheese sandwiches,
icy blue water among black slopes. Noting a strange hirsute nodding flower
that hangs. Why is the lake called 'Tristaina'?

If I were a hawk I'd sail over the mountains and the cities beyond
getting messages on the wind from outside my territory.
And I'd bear my tension across the air, balance on the gale
and swerve across the current and under to my base, my heart space,
under the world. Where the calm people drew pictures.

Water pours from the high lakes over shallow ledges
and trails down the valleys, accumulating substance from side streams.
Constantly balanced, it rattles the stones and excavates a route,
the shortest possible, through rocky landscapes unceasingly.
Linear arenas unfold, long troughs of grass and pale bedding planes
with a stone hut beside the stream, the door unlocked.
The water passes on and over the next step to flowery meadows
where horses graze, and small marshes spread
to the sides among trees. We are there, we agreed to fall.

Increased volume. Increased speed. No gain. Hold on to what we trust,
simple connections, result, truth, words we still use. Clear water in channels
falls down the valley, tumbling among trees to El Serrat,
which I misspelled in 1972 and has since been removed. I think I cope
better these days than I did then. Cosmic scope and epic trope
no longer trouble my sleep. They never meant anything
but power, but grabbing a space. The bottle is half full we share it.
The man behind the bar doesn't know where he is. 'Yes, I think
there used to be a village, they knocked it down to build the hotels.
I just work here in the season.' It is something else, the failure.
It is not us. Nothing can stop the war merchants now.
Clear moving swiftly water sliding down.

Pouring down the valley between the magnetic mountains
and we fall alongside, easy walking, fate grant us to float
many years yet thus along the earth holding a future in our eyes.
In 1956 there were peasants working in the fields here
who looked up and waved at English schoolboys, the road
was earthen and a passing car shrouded us in dust. They won,
outright, the cars, the professionals, the dream merchants,
they tear through the world. We maintain a vocabulary and a future
glimpsed through cracks, globed in tears at the eye rim,
waiting to descend. We shall not revert writing back to writing.
Llorts (next place) looks like a village but isn't, is all new,
and not for working people. Not indeed for anyone.
The higher professions take up the space and never use it.
Tax evasion draws an iron wall over the distances. We, what
are we among it but passing results of cheap oil?

If I were a hawk I'd rouse my red feathers and not be allured.
If I were a raven I'd sit on the roof of the new apartment block
and sing 'koax koax' to the empty rooms. If I were
a lammergeier I'd just hang around in the sky waiting for lunch
thinking 'Do what you like with your beautiful mountains,
but try to fear only the fearful and spare a thought for the fallen.'
Then I'd swoop and tear.

Amors de terra lonhdana, long-distance love, brought us here
and sustains us through the toil, of long-distance walking, of
short-distance confrontation with modernity. Let us therefore
open a bottle of Spanish wine we deserve it. And let us open it
at the breeze-block restaurant of the campsite at Ansalonga
with roast rabbit and chips. There we are safe from our own accusations
and what we wish sleeps in an inner pocket. It is a little cold
but the ambience is nested. Can we go any further down than this?
Is it really possible to reach the capital, the biggest megastore of all,
the Tesco of Divine Wrath? The bottle smiles, we haven't got far to go now.
The cook wishes us well and the river outside escorts us to our bags.

During the night bangs and a roaring, which mean differently here
from what they do in Lebanon, but we share a condition, of
having been betrayed. The small thin walls of a tent
protect us from whatever is outside. We survive the night, as some don't,
and emerge into day. Sometimes you meet a bright person in a lowly job
like the woman running the camp office, who tells you exactly what goes on,
how this country has no society. 'There's nobody much here

but migrant workers and absent owners.' An unreal structure, but
very expensive. Who pays for it? In the high hills yesterday
it was more than real it was the planet itself. It comprehended the city,
the forests of columns, the starred vaults under which true governance
improvises. Coffee at the breeze-block shed and on we go,
gently reluctantly downhill towards the Century of Massacres.

Of which we've had one and it looks like we're going to have another
for nothing, for nothing can stop the war merchants now,
with their little smiles, mouthing a dialectic. I remember Ordino
when it was a place. Our building is a razing, our concord is a rift.
What's left of Ordino doesn't seem to work, though it is
twice the size it was. But the air works, a mountain air coursing
down the vale like silver hounds and calling our thoughts back
to the unforgettable zones, where quasi human ravens
make their nests and croak freely the madrigals of love and war.
Outside the surviving food shop it works my hair into spandrels.

The mountains are still with us, we still bear, dry now,
the wounds they inflicted, the pain of the sensible,
the memories strung to it. The little town still mounts
on pedestrianised streets towards the sky.
[Eros] 'shook my heart like the wind flying down a mountainside'
into fir trees, aeolian harp of the world, songs of yearning. Not
an emptiness, not at all an emptiness, is the wilderness song
that follows us down to the town but a florescence of many lives
from which that thought grows, which 'doesn't stop at words, but flies on'
into the veracity ('blue') of the sky.

The plants on the tops of the mountains flower on our breath,
the gentians and the tulips, when we breathe the language clear
and benign, *media vita*. Also in the middle of a small town in the hills
every feature of which would wreck the vocabulary of pure poetry.
Come with your cappuccinos and your bus stops and your many
many empty flats and be a compositional impediment from which
to launch ourselves into metropolitan ardour, armed with alpine petals,
small and friable mountain cups. In brief, we catch a bus

towards retail immensity and immense indifference
to the bloody wars that pull at our centres.
Foc te ardâ, lume-amarâ – Let the fire burn you, bitter world
and burn away the dreams that cling to your surface, image deals
for the walls of your empty homes. The bus rattles on, concerned, politely,
to get us somewhere. The valley opens to a vast theatre of earth,
ridge upon ridge towards Spain, soaring over the wires.

A 'fiscal paradise' lies before us. What will you do, fiscal angels,
when apocalypse comes knocking at your door, and there's
no one in? The valleys tilt, the churches turn blue, everything
slides to the left corner and falls into a hole
(which is but a voice and darkness invisible).

———————

The central zone of building and development, the growth hole. The capital.

There's no one here. Memory of a voice round the corner, silence
of the tall blocks. The city is our wilderness. Shamans transport human
[spirit
to the arctic hells of the finance market, to become an animal.

Tallness has destroyed everything. Things stand alone, in masses.

No one has written on these walls *Sonos eternos jóvenes rebeldes!*

Music hidden in stone.

Leaning in fear towards the threshold of the Arab world.

Again a bright person in a lowly job, managing a small coffee-bar under
the tall walls, who explains the place is run by migrants, and bought by
[visitors.
Is this the dark voice at the foot of the stairs? But brightly she explains
that in some way 'the nature' keeps us going and a future ahead, a work to
[be done
and a pact with sociality. A dawn thing, when all the dreams fall off.
A hard time for the heart, but 'We are proud of our tears.'
Then how do we face the spread of harm? When our hands
reach out to the power glades they grasp a vacuum.

There were ethics, among all classes, maintained from generation
to generation by the means available to the group, to acknowledge
common humanity and locate blame precisely in the structures of harm.
Neither the European wars nor the *Daily Mail* could entirely destroy them.
There were discussions on street corners in Salford after the pubs were
[closed,
men in flat hats and white scarves deciding not to sack the Jewish shop
and not to listen to the media campaign against Muslims and not to be afraid.

Heart, how can you not break down, that your love
is shrunken to four walls, and everything outside is delivered
to the empties? They have taken over the whole public world, where desire
planted a garden, and they have built a car-park on it
and nothing can stop them now. But the airs and the
electricity circulate on the mountain tops and things are remembered
that protect us against destructive certainty. A slow history accumulates in
[those
parts of the world that remain true to themselves, and forget the whole.
The tall hole. *Heart speak or die.*

Give payment and thanks and go. It is time for some sanity. We catch
[another bus,
to El Pas de la Casa, which is absolutely insane, and another, to
[L'Hospitalet, where
French shopkeepers struggle with enormous sacks of cheap goods on the
[station platform
like the damned of the 4th bowge, and the train goes through the mountains
and across the plain, to Toulouse, and dinner. I notice the word *Ospita*
contained in L'Hospitalet as I sit at a pavement table with cassoulet.
It concerns me. How could the world think without its soul? Always if
you look for it there is something curative, the words held in the seeds
scattered on the mountain slopes, far away, waiting patiently for winter.

Music released by stone. Fully declared whatever the options.

The threshold of the Arab world, if Lebanon could be saved.

Ordinary and orderly, acts and failures, tipping the heart cradle.

Aria with Small Lights

Late one summer evening in 1997 I walked out onto the hillside at the back of an Italian mountain village, and soon after I'd passed the last house noticed a glow in the air ahead of me among conifers, which proved to be the small village cemetery. The glow was from the lights on the graves, some of them candles but mostly small electric lights of the kind we use for Christmas trees. The cloud base was almost on the ground and the light although slight was dispersed into it as a luminous mist. I walked up to the gate and stopped. In the following poem this action of approach is repeated, by my reckoning, thirty times, in almost every stanza, figurised in many different ways but always as an approach to an area which is not entered, before which action is suspended.

—oOo—

At an ordinary life I walked one night
on the high ridge top, Vitiana, great valley
of the Serchio north of Lucca. I walked,
nobody about, late evening, stone ginnels
and steps, enormous toads and fireflies, warm
darkness, I walked up behind the village.
There was a glow round a corner. In the hand
of the night haze I wasn't anyone, I had
no history, some kind of foreigner under a wall.

And anyone could become this. There was a light
dispersing into the darkness above a gate in a wall,
a glow hovering in the space I walked towards
nameless and unknown under lit windows
on small tracks past the top of the village, harm
strapped to my back so it was a needed message
I walked towards, a diagnosis, it was a land I
petitioned to enter at the custom shed but had
no language, no history of known good at all

because I refused to be reminded and might yet
meet a new mind in a night glow hovering tall
over me in the under branches of a few low trees,
not moving at all but hanging there like police notices
in an occupied city, the blue light you have to turn
under and in the door to bow before the empty page
and ask if you might be considered worthy to stand
to the side of this country, under the wall, with no bad
words spoken against you the pure eyed calf in its stall,

20

standing there while the cemetery glows, and hides its bite.
When I reached the gate in the wall it became further
to what was in front of me than all I had known, the cot
of continuing, because it was a town and nothing else
a town with all its lights below me alive and burning
through the night it was the very town of death
busy about its businesses telephoning across the land
balancing its currencies against its goods and I had
nothing to offer it. I had nothing to offer it at all.

I was halted before it, I was in a life in the night
not worth telling while traces of my father
still hung about me. We were living in a hut
or cottage off the village square somewhere. Thence
we walked thence we loved so we drank the stinging
wine. In the early evenings the people who were
really there sang in the square gathered in a band.
There were flesh hooks in their song, there were knives
to cut life out, there were eyes fastened to the wall,

the walls that hang over you with small lights
in small windows near their summits. I'd rather
shrink to a blob of sweat on the road under that
towering domus than claim a thing I never so
much as lived a week in. Or be a ghost entering
people's houses quietly through the closed door
a thread of ink through lives, out the back and
walk on up to the cemetery, whose lights are knives,
at which day trades recoil, though gentle and small.

The colourless lights, burning in the night
like points of certainty in a page of weather
and the only certain thing left us, is that
message from a great distance across the snow
and ice of death to this warm night burning
with one meaning. Which if I could stress forth
on the tables of pasture I'd be able to stand
the silence. I can't stand the silence, the sad
messages reaching no one at all,

the vacuum at the desk across which no fight
and no love can pass, and is set there for
us to make some moment of, and know a lot
less. Leaning over the gate I ceased to know
where love can hide, someone's name burning
like a fag-end on the path, and remain sure
of the pavement under all lives. The walled
garden with the lights of nothing on the ground
was the end of my thin days in liberty hall.

So I stepped no further forward than I might
and there were fireflies coding hope and loss: where
are you this dark night hovering in and out
of the bean frames on the rich hillside and slow
toads moved with infinite patience and no harm
on the village steps under the dim lamps. The dark space
behind the church had a lit shrine in the wall that fed
the roots of separation. Where are you all this grand
pulp of living night so educative and tall?

Big soft harmless toads, I suppose, in slow flight
from untoadness, as I from the shadow of my father.
You from difference, as I from like. Reaching this summit
graveyard full of lights piercing the softness what else
could I be but someone peering out of a small window frame
at a human distance unsuspected, like Thomas Gray faced
with the university of the tilled ground, and appalled and
made to sing against everything he had ever owned,
What are these, who suddenly seem so educated and tall?

who shine at their stations in silence, dressed bright
as royalty. What are these shades behind lethal wire
dressed in stripes and meeting at a point of light, that
cannot speak, so we are safe from, but whose houses
evidently have a party going on and we are not invited.
Like the singing in the square and the lights in the shrine,
like the wedding funeral. We are privileged to stand
to the side and let the procession past, we are not so bad
as to deny the signal of a strict fate during a fancy ball.

And I am truly amazed, I come from a sorry place
far away and still I know that these points of cold fire
are lives given wholly into where they are, so that
they can never be anywhere else but like a mouse
in the wainscot or a toad on the road eat the same
bread in a different country and trade the same love
strife in a different light. We are holes in this light, and
we are strangers in this country, which takes my hand
and leads me to the graveyard metricating my drawl.

This walled orchard no one can enter without pass
and currency, without name. Yet I walked without fear
into the Campo at Pisa (I had paid) and faced what
silenced thought, leaving nothing but a pause
in the night a faint shuffle on the road avoiding blame
as avoiding love. Piled arcades the shade of a dove
wrapped energy in care at every grain of the land
overflowing with need. And I one of many had hauled
my soul to that construct, glowing pale and ready to fall.

Mother rosebush, share my dark red glass
like a sentence in the silence, a tension where
the buds burn in the night, burn to a point that
points me out as a stranger. Therefore silent, because
somewhere between cash and corpse I lost my name
or avoided it, and stood in the field of honour: above
me the timely circles turned in white stone and
wrote me to the new horizon like a train on the hard
lines at night, bright signals before the long haul.

Mother ashes, grande dame, where now is all that fuss?
all that patting and parting, the tremors in the air
as the lamb is led past the mutton shed with its bat
and ball and its brain in a satchel for the next course
where is all that fear? O it's here, here and same,
here at a scatter of points which is all I shall have
to die with, when I agree to die I shall thrust my hand
in this pocket full of hard-won reward and cast
it to the sky. The burial lights wrap absence in a shawl.

But I twisted out of the village grip, the college hand-
shake, on a curled path above the massed houses. There
was a stone wall, behind the wall a glow and a gap
in the wall and in the gap a gate. I felt like a horse
fastened to a cart awaiting instruction, tug of rein
this way or that into some known domain of love
that would deliver us from the unknowable land
of certainty, icy and far. I leaned on the barred
gate as a dumb beast in need of honest toil.

What I needed was a mobile phone to hold in my hand
and signal like the fireflies floating in the warm dark air
signalling love, then signalling death. Tick and tap,
fruition and destruction by a slight variant of morse,
buzz, croak, death is the cost of every song we gain.
So chatting on the line as usual and the world like a dove
flutters away from our self-cancelling discourses and
leaves me standing alone on the dark ground starred
with former lives, trying not to believe that they call.

But they do, as the fireflies call with their fire and
the slow toads with their patience and my life where
it comes full circle will call and call to you, What
can I bring to your lowly stall, from the endless pause
called hope? If I could bring the truth I would be a pain
in your side, an unwelcome immigrant in the office
for questioning. And I stand outside in the dark land
signalled to by the people I knew when I was a proud
witness to human goodwill, wrapped in my pall.

They are no longer with us and their thoughts stand
in remote places blinking off and on in bare
corners of the night to whoever passes and waits,
thoughts that welcome the stranger as matter of course.
Someone is willing to take the dark and narrow lane
and meet the shine of a dark face eyes into eyes
as a mutual trust and if proved wrong let it stand
as a priority. And say so and say it out loud –
the dead cannot speak less than the objective whole,

speak it gently in small lights, candles and christmas bulbs
strung, rose-mother, in your garden kitchen, where
the night cakes are forced. Held in your skirts they
smoke towards dawn. And here, wishing the cause
of anxiety to be known, but to remain apparently sane,
I cast my futures on a spangled board. It would be nice
to make some connection there, for my number to land
on a fruiting point, a windfall. I turn to face the portal, add
an arm to a shoulder and we sing together the songs of shortfall.

Facing the music, the gleam in the fiddler's eye, as we must,
me and my ghostly other we fill our lungs with air
arm on shoulder each to each and openly declare
our immense disappointment, and deep sense of loss.
The details are unimportant. The tune is again
in the minor, to a slow rocking four. And not a trace
of gloom shadows our faces, boldly we face the band
in the triumph of our time on earth to have and hold
the music that sits across pain, curved with the earth and as loyal.

It's me and my double-ganger in duet, a bit of rust
in the pipes but never mind, the people are out there
tiaras and tie-pins twinkling in the mist, in the smoke that
rises from the stage lights we sing of beauty and old wars.
The sky is solidly behind us, day's tincture on the wane
as night pulls from ridge to ridge its pierced surface,
its black furnace, over us all. Together we sink, and
sing the stars to ground in our decline. Pulling the earth hood
over our faces, we burn to nothing behind the wall.

Almost nothing. Some pieces or tokens of mutual trust
gleam on the earth, and read as a transcript of care
across organised cruelty. And these are things that
we have always had, for which we owe nothing because
we are already there where success is in vain, where
patience nests in the fruiting trees and a fine lace
of stars hangs round the neck and illumines the face
of the sleeping worker. I creep in beside him and
together we sound the night's distances in the blood-
beat brother to brother, Simon and Paul.

It would be good to get it exactly right for once
before we part for ever and wander away where
the rivers touch the sea full of shadows waiting
to return. Not to get it wrong, the passionate force
that speaks us while we're here and speaks us fair
if we deserve it, shining in the night like old bone,
the corner against harm. It would be a fine grace
to issue wholesome energy forth but here this grand
sequence of goodwill collapses, I don't know what good
all this wishing does, I don't know where to crawl

and hide, from the accusing fires. 'You might
in some court or school, get away with asking. Here
you have to answer.' But it would be a good thing
surely, to view the earth-flares with gladness or the
sky-fires with resignation, or simply to stand there
in the mist the flames of distance on all sides and gain
from somewhere a willingness while the sun's
in hiding, to let this darkness be. It's yours, in your hand
squirming with shining lives like small prawns cooked
in white wine. Love these delicate creatures and eat them all.

It's yours, the voices say, the voices in the night vat,
the candles on the birthday cake, warming the black air
under the small trees on the top of the hill, singing
far behind the wall, Somewhere a voice is calling.
What is mine? – Anything you care to name,
as long as you don't move, while peace holds this fair
prospect is yours. And up here nothing moves from base
to zenith all is still. Isn't this then the very land
you wanted to enter? Doesn't this motionless moment hold
a four-way tension across the world? So they call

from far away, from deep under the tricks of light.
And I'm still here at the gate, seeing from afar
the small flames of history like a traveller pausing
at the top of the pass to view the burning houses
of the home valley. That was my uncle's, that was where
we first met, that was the school, and the whole frame
is split for ever. I have gained this empty place
full of darkness and energy points. From my hand
it falls like sand but I remember yesterday's gold
light on the white arch, distinctly, each in all.

Old light, Italian, passing into the stone as I sat
there paused in a personal shade where
slow toads walk and funeral candles burn, causing
an absence in the day, a blink in the light which is
full of history and tracks all deaths and sorrows. There
in the burning light on the sculpted portal the lost names
file in at the door on a hopeless quest for peace
and belonging, refused point blank at every office and
no reason, for there is none. We shrug. We have sold
the light to the tourists and wait with candles in the black hall.

A book, about war and death, is open at a black page with white
punctuation. But all I can read is the story of a lost partner,
an old man in Dorset seeking the art of forgetting
in slow sung syllables before dawn. How does this
help the southern victims of corporate greed? The air
holding the light says it does, says that blame
disperses like a silver cloud in the night and ceases
all its clamour. Then the song is slowly sung, the band
wrapping it in distance saying we shall all when we are old
turn our losses on a silver palate under a dry wall.

And how does that help the victims of massive corporate
indifference? Oh it does, says the tidal rhythm, care
is balanced on a sense of what you are and the thing
you will finally be. What are you going to be? – this
old fellow walking slowly up to the graveyard where
his memories are errant fireflies and a single name
fills both staves? Or some tight bag of successes
counting its gains in the broken backs and foiled
lives of a continent, happy as a pike in a waterfall.

Life's own loss and failure truly owned will be a pride
to inhabit in some corner of the earth, a sorrow where
the new earth pivots. And some creature will sing
it forth – not the bearer, not the old man on the hill, this
pleasure falls to the reader, the lurker behind, whose care
for distance inhabits the loss, whose truth came
and stood by the widower at the grave. Caresses
of 1965 are set in a nosegay and placed on the ground.
Turns and heads for home without a sound.

Shining Cliff

In December 2006 my daughter celebrated her 30th birthday in an isolated hostel in Shining Cliff Wood, near Ambergate, Derbyshire, among twenty of her friends. A few months later I wrote these reminiscences of the woods, which are involved in questions of future trust precipitated by the occasion, questions that are normally difficult to reach.

—oOo—

Forfeit world and win
the shred of earth that spells true
that wills itself through common need

Keep it for ever if you can. When you are 80
meet here again and take the same oath
in each others' eyes.

The robin hesitating on the gate,
the blackbird peering into the grass.

*

Crossing the small wooded valley
knowing the world's instability, learning
the colour of its fade, to keep a record

For ever if you can, meeting
and passing signs to the future
long after any of your birthdays.

A different robin on the gate,
blackbird on the young elder.

*

Meet across the world's divides
and there is your shining,
where it has always been

Through the night closure (cunning world)
and the future when you will move slowly
supported on frames

With birds to cheer your way then as
now calling under brittle leaves.

*

Hope engendered in company
sorrow's picture staring down
the long song against despair

Secure your beautiful white hair
we shall not always linger here, scooping
fluff from the machines. Listen,

The thrush at its limit, the totally
unreasonable wren, piping through the gates of death.

*

The long high song echoing
over the trees down the slope
the leaves flicker a world picture

A tempered wish, a tied purpose
slices the air, our failing
falling ecstasy, our trade.

The caged goldfinch, a memory of Baghdad,
robin and blackbird suddenly flown.

*

The ring in the air, the green mottled light
moving on the side of your face, you will
have to insist on this validation

For fifty years through all the exits and ignorance
star and leaf in tension through the sky
as the mist descends, and

The ring is not for love now, the ring
is for war. You know this and continue,
arm over the magpie's shoulder.

*

Birches and small oaks. Fear and anger
stirring in the wind, which is not strong,
swaying like warblers on reeds, we make our progress

In slow careful steps, over and through
the barriers the world creates towards
horizons of thought, purple patches on leaves

And off you go, on your own as we all were,
sorrow band across the forehead, opening the gates,
the birds flock over the stones.

*

Bright surety here where it always was,
flying on unsure wings
to perch high on the world's lack.

We forget it, fumbling
with connectors at the edge
of our spaces as the days roll over.

Starlings and blackbirds
high in the trees, presiding there
where the president failed.

*

Down in the valley below high in the clouds the old tension
is stretched that snaps into love and hatred, red leaf,
put these cares in your portfolio.

We edge between our failures
some of our failures are vast enough to blanket the world
and hope survives as a heartlight calculated on the dark earth
a point gathering others, small fires dotted on the plain.

Keep them burning into the next century,
you old drunks.

*

The pristine burn of thought that
rends up from the stones
what must be done

The earth must be recognised
The dead must arise and the washing up must be done but first of all
the earth must be recognised

And when recognised released.
Tell it to the astounded pigeon. That bangs
into flight.

*

December, patches of bracken stalks
brown leaves clinging to some of the trees
and strewn in the pale grass, thousands
of chestnuts rotting on the ground

The A6, slightly visible, slightly audible
down the end of the valley through the trees
your route home to southern business.
Remember this north before its bitterness.

Hairclips, Cuban rap, analysis
And a farewell to the song thrush.

*

In five months' time flowers will start to emerge
on the ground and in the trees
but none of us will be here then

We'll be somewhere else
pursuing our centres
to the world's core and closure

With passion to reach the world's
gravity. For they exist,
the little ones with nothing to eat.

Bright eye, yellow beak.

*

How then should I your true love know
from another one?

A voice, a message, a promise,
a wrong to be righted, a future
moving in the forest at night
towards a conclusion, and an end to oppression.

May he reach you from the ends of the earth,
humming-bird caught in his hair.

Best at Night Alone

version of 15 January 2011

In 2007 we stayed for several days in an isolated house in Haute Provence near the village of Montsallier. I spent most of the late evenings there sitting at a table near a window, reading, writing, and listening to music. The window showed only darkness and faint sky lines, with some lights from the village in the distance. The next week we moved to a flat we had rented on the edge of the village of Faucon, to the east of Vaison-la-Romaine. The window I sat at here in the late evenings looked down onto the road at the base of the village lit by orange streetlights, with a few lit windows and small vistas of the stone of the village rising to its hilltop centre before me. From another window there was, in the daytime, a view of the north face of Mont Ventoux. The writing from these places took under its wings a number of other situations in which I have sat by a window in the late evening, especially Tony Baker's house in Wirksworth and my own house in Cambridge, and as the house and window multiplied, so did the person who was sitting there, becoming various ages and conditions from one moment to the next, all worried about different things. This began immediately, with someone probably from the Near East, evidently ill or wounded, who returned several times – I called him 'the refugee'. Another was the self-taught French botanist and entomologist Pierre Henri Fabre, and there were others, including some interloping French poets, and finally a Swedish poet who refused to go away, or go to sleep, and almost took over the whole thing.

—oOo—

Night long over fields and hills the dome turns.
Lit window, figure bent over table, forest
edge star traces contracted on a point of harm,
biting the bone. Where are my people?
Cowering under desert shadows. Children laugh.

*

The window figure blocks the light,
dark form in a pale frame, pain
courses through the body as a bequest of the total.
The wooded hills, the night birds sitting
silent on the stones, dark auditors of random violence.
Families torn apart. Love's revenge
falls on the children.

*

Pain in the chest, in the memory,
a distant street lamp suddenly goes out.
My vanishing point. Dark wind
and the thrashing of branches, rain
on the glass. My home's validation.

*

Me with my alcohol and fat. I remember better days,
why are we living out here in this shadow land
driven from our pasturage or choral fate, our tale
a thin script thrust into the night
across fields of lavender, ecstatic proteins
burning into lives. My sweet poison.
My working timetable.

*

All our resources gone to
waste in the desert, these people are
wrecking the earth.

And nowhere but here in these patient groves
will an eyelid be opened to the earth's curve
at dawn or fall of night.

No, I don't want a sandwich.
I don't want a valet case.

*

Street, street, banal street
paved with promises the mind
walks you in the middle of the night,
and a hand is held out, cupped I am
busy with my insects, truth and
hope, hand reaching for hand.
A knock at the door. Two
children run away down the street
laughing, hand in hand.

*

A white poplar
spread against the grey sky.

A vast, silent, military vocabulary
a map spread on the ground.

Great webbing of white letters
falling to earth
where they lie ill and dying.

*

Upland slopes full of spiked plants, October
skeletons rattling themselves in the night.
A message forms at the lips' limit. What is left
of our liberty but a scatter of aggressive bones?
and very disgruntled populations liable to
paranoid acts.

Moths at the window.
The home that survived resentment.
The home that survived alcohol and fat.
The home that survived encryptment.
Needing help to climb the stairs.

*

The great mountain forms erased at night,
no more lights, no more houses. How could there
not be paranoia in such a place as this,
threatened by the world brokers at every act? Shouts of
Freedom and Democracy, shatter people's bones.
Beacon darkness through the fields, where
the children are hiding.

*

'We have thrown away everything worth having
and erased everything worth knowing
and now we are bombing Eden.'

Lord God, you who made me,
turn me into a pillar of black salt
for the soldiers to practise shooting at.

Moths on the windows, serious and symmetrical,
moths with purpose. When I open the windows
the moths fill the room the whole
pillar of alienation suddenly opens like a winter rose
and all the company of song.

*

(after Deguy)
Singing old songs together in the evening
like nomads round the camp fire. The rare
moment when we agree to die
it is Orpheus, it is the soft thing stronger
than stone, stronger than tree or
scattered creatures, the song in its clearing
as one by one we stand and leave
in good order by the law of random numbers.

They have all gone to bed and left me here.
Singing old songs together in the evening.

———————

And where does all this get us where do we go from here where are my glasses
what are the practicalities of collective hope? Motives removed from history
collect like insects in a glass bottle shake it and the bombs fall. They fall like
rain on the mountainside nobody knows why they are falling they think it is
something natural like rain some order of the world. The world is entirely
out of this committee humming over an elegant couple-dance. And there will
be too, when the gain stops.

*

When the gaining stops
we shall all gain some peace
and a space in which to operate
the mechanisms that grow from the
first movement of thought, the goodwill
lodging on the lip, lacking a word, the ancient
honeyed madness.
Hope sleeps there, the quiet place,
corners of matt stone on the dark hill
while the Burmese singer
plucks our sleep.

*

If you want, the war can stop. If you want enough. All you have to do is want
and it will, all of it. But only that, only all of it, not some favour, not some
dream. Sing the slow long song and watch the forces part. Street, street,
baleful street, paved with wishes, I don't set foot on you any more, my legs
ache, I climb inside and contract onto the point of harm.

*

Singing the old songs I
cut the writing across time
as the mountain edge cuts the sky
as if I wished to die.
The buzzards overhead searching
for a possible incision it is their duty
not ours.

*

The founder of Situationism dies of red wine in a farmhouse deep in the
French countryside. Once you see it, he says, you have won. What do you
on earth do when you've won? Make silence speak.

*

Worries in my hair like midges, buzzing and
getting lost among trees and fading to distance,
Mars, Venus, dusk on earthen spring,
the great fruiting vastness beyond these walls
all the people living their lives and I cannot address
less than that, some favour or dream. Only you listen
are my opening eye, piercing the lights.
Venerable honeyed lips, bitter wine.
Earth's glories reclaimed.

*

The area round the house is a mass of dry grasses with insects moving around.
The hills beyond covered in small oak trees, east-west ridges extending from
Greece to Spain. Far away to the left over the fields the village very little
inhabited now, a few street lights at night. Lavender fields, harvested, strips
of dark stubble and heaps of underbush awaiting burning. A dormouse
scratches in the roof. The Colorado beetle is said to have shown itself in the
Beaujolais and there are *mites de nourriture* in the flour bin. We are careless
and discordant with our alcohol and fat, and other powers.

*

Help me up the stairs to bed
I have had enough
of my own skill, it
strangulates me I think I am right to say
that there is hope in the world
if you look, in especially those parts
of the world where people shelter under
shadows it is there. The poets
dream of honour but hope
is self-propagating.

*

How the wind outside rolls against the house, and in the skylight pale clouds
move across, a blanket drawn across the sky, but that too moves on and then
there is only that empty depth, with two points, two bright eyes staring down.
They stare and stare but they can't see us in here. But still they stare.

*

Mind going out into the world to seek its objects
speaking back. What then is this *grimoire* this
obstruction on the table? I close it and fetch the wine
which as Baudelaire said sings in the bottle
of the whole, of the redress. As the truth sings in the book.

*

(after Bonnefoy)
Night with its greens and its blues and a bit of dark red curdling the bottom
of the page. Quickly I write the word tear, then star. I write birth. I write
shepherds and three wise men. I write the bulb has gone and it's dark.

*

So we can begin. Groping round in the dark
bumping into furniture. The 'things of this world'
are here somewhere.
Biting back.
Singing together in the evening.

———————

Floral wreaths attached to a lamp post.

Take me home, country roads.

———————

The two stars, cat's eyes in the void
one of them moves, the other
suddenly goes out and I'm groping in the dark
for the things of the sky. The children
know me, they think I'm a funny old thing.

*

(Carol)
Like the wren I lie in care's bed at my solstice.
Tiny bird, preferring darkness, heart
beats 450 /min. at rest, unlikely
to survive the winter.
Still under thorn Under shadow.

The robin brings alcohol and fat
the three wise men bring useless presents
the shepherds bring nothing but themselves
and the possibility of a future where
nor you nor we nor anybody
bound the world into its suffering.

*

Wide open spaces of patience
gloss with light the faint opening wing.
I watch the caterpillars die in a ring.
It is not a tragedy. They were learning to sing.

*

Darkness, that is not a human condition
but a condition of the earth, that renders us
isolated and uniquely empowered at
a turning point and if we are quick and careful
before the light returns in the silence when
people sleep because they think there is nothing to see
there we can reverse the world's drift by
a spasm of thought carried across several mountains
like fire in a fennel stalk. And a bluish paleness
from the night horizons.

*

Despair declines and a birth is anticipated,
the dark shadow covering the hill dissolves into the ground
and there is hope where hope cannot be, hard against the earth,
out in the fields of vengeance. Because a sequence has begun
which must continue, is bound to it, through the black light of
nameless states.

*

Do but listen to the Bushmen music and the space is changed,
immediate completion on minimal resource
and nothing is hidden from us, nothing is coded,
evidence fills the space we inhabit in its
night show, blue seeking into brown and creating green
leaves scattered on the threshold, unconditional welcome.

*

High window onto the narrow street, a few local lads
are larking around down there the estate agent's window
shines. I'm separated from my library and if
any of my days offers the world an answer I
don't know which one.

High mind-bid for the present condition like
birdsong mounting to a spherical estate not
for sale where the beautiful pages shine on the
edge of a life like a Mexican harp band that
knows where it's going.

*

Night corners, orange light on matt stone
in small stadia on the hillside whose edge
is lost into the sky, and some lit windows.

And there I sat, and there I stayed
and there I heard them sighing like
stars in the sky when the winter birds come over

And dark wings fold us into the earth
for night is our site and there we suit
our brows to the waiting clay.

*

The bigger the powers that combine to split the earth the stronger the local
discourse that takes no notice of them. But mounts lanterns on the awning
and books the musicians for next Friday and gets the big pots out of storage.
They know exactly what is happening in the high offices and make sure that
the music is level with the earth, in case of gunfire.

*

In night corners small fires glow, travellers warm their limbs, there is food and drink and some tired dance movements are made. People cast out of their land, human flesh degraded against steel, gather in corners of vacant lots and face each other across a dark emptiness, a fulcrum of harm, a blueprint of corporate loyalty.

*

Bushmen, the most persecuted people on earth, persecuted continuously for three hundred years and still persecuted, relentlessly and mercilessly persecuted as if they must at all costs be driven to nonentity and the world must be finally rid of the few, powerless and harmless, that are left. As if we cannot possibly have this tiny population crouched in the semi-desert eking a living and maintaining a form of wisdom almost entirely beyond us, that sends the mind out into the world to encounter the world's terms rather than taking the opportune thought-course that absorbs the surplus. And they know that God is vile and sense him out there in the darkness seeking their harm. They could teach us, few and scattered and night-cornered, of us, as we are, but we discard them.

*

(after Ekelöf)
Best alone at night with the secretive lamp I hear
the whisper of forest like a passing ship, more alone even
than in hospital and day after day the same discomfort,
everybody's, that nobody shares. Half elsewhere
I turn back to the night 'His face is the blue shadow
of his hand' this ink life that takes me across the old cities dissolving
smoke into the air and veer into the future.

———

The red blind is down and all I know beyond the window is a faint rumbling noise, with a fainter hiss attached to its edge. This is the turning wheel whose moment speaks of love. And we don't want this love. We shut it out of the house and return to a solitude with eyes in our hands, that are cast to the night.

*

> The things of the world, shouted in the world
> *We are civilians. What have we done?*
> Succession, sacrifice, solution, words
> that hiss across the world like oil figures.
>
> It would have been better to forget. There are
> forms of lament that nurture harm. Obediently
> forget, as the eaves drip into snow and the lamp expires.

*

Alone in quiet night will be my best pseudonym, absent from any centre. And I shan't know better than anybody else, why should I want to? My hair grey, my eyes brown.

*

> Referred back to the lives of those who work,
> in graveyard and ballroom across the land
> from worm to star and back the entire dome
> sounds in chorus for someone
> has again placed a medal on a small earth feature
> positioning an earthen future on the thin thread
> of light the horizon's opening pain to a
> wide meadow full of positive force.

*

The darkness that surrounds the heart, with a line of light in the far distance where the world enters, cautiously. Gentle murmurings of liver lungs and intestines, calming the heart, keeping the dream music going, singing *Heart of my heart...*

So the heart, flattered, won't notice the world as it comes slowly and cautiously through the door and won't kill it.

*

Ekelöf 1932
I shan't sleep tonight.
Forgive me if I write badly.
Forgive me if I write stupidly.
Death was ignored, and sat there
like some hapless employee.

The bands of night circle the house
the wind hisses on the gables
the circular graveyard
turns slowly in the night.
If I am wrong, forgive me.

Memory of a plume of thought
brushing down the hillside like snow
announcing the human victory
and purpose bursts out of enclave.
He gets up and opens the window.

*

These pieces are written quickly, with long periods between them during
which they are not looked at or thought of, except that a beginning, an *incipit*,
may come from nowhere late in the evening alone and quiet and it is rarely
more than a disturbing sound, a scrape beyond a wall, a creak, a low bump,
a cradle sound.

*

All I ever wanted, a hand touches a wooden table
And there is nothing to pay, looking at the hills
Through the window and hearing a faint cry from
The cradle, remembering a carved stone at Southwell

Of intricately entwined leafage: somebody was capable
Of setting aside the world's catalogue of ills
And I wanted a lot more than that, a cat's dream
in a quiet basket, of the great fix, the claw in harm.

The claw passes through air and retracts
At the delicate stone edge, the world stands
Alone not knowing what it wants,

An elite or an egalitarian structure. Call it home,
Let it settle round us and hope the wild fires don't
Reach it. There's nothing else either to want or own.

*

These hearts always at war,
Twenty years day and night.

O Earth you don't listen, you don't understand,
You don't speak when you see me dying.
O Earth you don't protect your children,
You don't lead them home from the killing fields
You just cry and cry.

Damn these years always at war.
Damn the liars who speak of community.

*

I am perched on the window-ledge waiting to get a connection. The faint
crust of earth betokens itself in wisps of gendering, that is to say, shyly. I
know that these whispers can break into gunfire when the contract is broken.
The contract is in the very far ends of the tree tips against the sky making
lens for star eyes. Making oculi for sincerity.

*

The greater the poverty the happier the children.
They sport on the boundaries of the killing fields, and
some don't last long. But are never bowed under the threat
of excellence. Our laments make them giggle.

And the insects and the art. The gunfire they greet
with mistrust, waiting to be told, and
may not wait long but escape from a world of threat
into their own excellence.

*

A church bell. The first bird signal: a note repeated anything from
four to fifteen times in random order. It starts to rain,
small circles on the river surface, there and gone.

O lullabye, my sweet little hopefuls, here is your ending.

Bits and Pieces Picked Up in April 2007
or
Six Days in Tuscany with Roger Langley

Sunday
The depth of incision into the stone: the degree of power exercised.
The balance and turn of the perceiving body, in attendance,
carved, light or deep, by the nervous system. There
shall be no rulers. We shall make our own ways.
In the middle, the three attendants hang their heads.

Monday
O world world, you disappoint us.
The gentle green hills and the forced labour.
Later reassured by
I gettatelli, the abandoned children,
the bronze angels that carry you into what you are.

Monday
Sienese: free play of detail within market-led formalities.
Perhaps not a very good idea.
Some of these Madonnas are nursing dolls or piglets!

Tuesday
Paradisal sight, which extends to infinity.
Arcades, stars, shadows, the eyes staring through us. There shall be
no more wars. The blood-light, the focus.

Wednesday
No mystery, no symbol.
We hope for messages.
The birds flock across the sky.

Wednesday
The great forehead, the downcast gaze,
the head held high, the rich lips,
the interior pain, that never dies, of this,
queen of this.

Thursday
Paradisal sight, halted at a wall
of blue-streaked marble.

Love as focused as my eye muscles can make it
to a sky-streaked terminal.

Thursday
A landscape which is a state of mind
but not always the same state of mind.

This evening a proud antagonism
an anchorage, in dark green grass.

A pause in anxiety,
A painting.

Friday
Elliptical settlements on hilltops with small churches.
Alternating bands of white and red stone.
Pigeon flutters in the tree-top,
serin sings from the thicket. Somewhere else,
sad dancing, in couples. There is
Only one end. A circular window
in a chequerwork of white and red stone.

The Twelve Moons

After Li Ho

Li Ho is now known as Li He (AD 790–816). He was a well-connected but entirely unsuccessful young man whose verse has been described as 'Dionysian' and so untypical in Chinese traditions. These versions were done in 1965 after those by Ho Chih-yuan in The White Pony *edited by Robert Payne (1949). A number of phrases remain only slightly altered from this source, including some which were evidently misreadings, and this is one reason for retaining the superseded transliteration as the name of a partly fictional poet. But in 2006 I made changes in the light of the more scholarly* The Poems of Li Ho *by J.D. Frodsham (1970), and the revised edition* Goddesses, Ghosts, and Demons: the collected poems of Li He *(1983). A mid-century enumerative ennui remains characteristic of the text but now scattered with points of figurative density and rhythmic disturbance resulting from the confrontation with more abstract and complicated interpretations of the Chinese characters. The poems were written as lyrics, and they supposedly note the seasonal changes (though it seems always to be cold) passing through the palace enclosures, and their various abandoned women. The thirteenth poem was in Frodsham's books only and is different in tone; the thirteenth month was the result of ministerial failure to co-ordinate solar and lunar calendars.*

—oOo—

First Moon

I climb the stone tower to watch spring arrive,
amber willow-buds, palace water-clock's slow drip,
mist spirals wander through the fields in cold
green light a dark wind leans over the grass.
    An embroidered bed bears her
    asleep at dawn, jade-cool skin,
      dewy eyelids closed buds to a paling sky.
On the road willow catkins not yet ready.
The flag leaves perhaps, before long.

Second Moon

Where they pick mulberries by the stream
we drink wine among dandelions and orchids.
Flag leaves crossed swords clash in scented air,
restless swallows scream at spring's demand,
green patches on rose-mist screening.

High-set hair and gold bird-tail
rivalling the evening clouds –
in pearl skirts she dances on wind-steps,
    at the ferry she says goodbye with *flowing river song*.
The drinkers' spines go cold,
south mountain dead.

Third Moon
East wind fills our brows with spring.
In flower-city willows darken, deep in the palace
wind stirs through bamboo, new green dancing skirts like water.
For hundreds of miles bright wind on wet clover
a warm mist blown down to earth.
        Slave girls waiting to follow armies
        apply careful eyeshade, red banners
        flapping on the walls of their compound,
        scents wafted over the river,
        fallen pear-blossom, autumn by proxy.

4th Moon
Cool at dusk and dawn, all the trees.
A thousand mountains, green depths beyond clouds,
faint scent in the rain falling through greenery,
leaves and round flowers beaming through garden doors.
Water sheds green ripples in stone ponds,
heavy late spring, blossom gladly falling,
old red flowers on the ground, glow in tree-shade.

Fifth Moon
Carved jade lintel, gauze hanging in the open doorway,
lead-bright water from the well,
ducks and drakes painted on fans.
        Snowy skirts dance in the cooled halls,
        sweet dews rinse the sky blue,
        silk sleeves balloon on the wind,
        beads of sweat on their bodies, precious grain.

Sixth Moon
Now they cut the raw silk
and split the dappled bamboo.
We lie on bamboo mats in frost silks
cool as autumn jade.

A flame-red mirror opens in the east,
a spinning cartwheel mounts the sky,
on fiery dragons the Red Emperor comes.

Seventh Moon
The milky way sheds cold across the sky,
round dew-drops on the stone bowls,
flowers appear at each twig end.
Old grass mourns dying orchids,
night sky paved with jade, leaves
on the lotus pond, green coins floating.
    She wishes her dancing-skirt were less thin,
    she feels cold on the flower-woven mat.
A morning wind sighs at dawn,
the Great Bear glittering stoops down the sky.

Eighth Moon
    Through the night the young widow grieves,
    the lonely traveller thinks of home.
Spiders spin silk on the beams,
a lamp on the wall sheds petals,
the room breathes its light into outer darkness,
tree shadows back-slant across windows.
Easily now dews drift down
and ornament the floating lotus flowers.

Ninth Moon
Fireflies lost in the summer palace, sky like water,
yellow bamboos, cold pools, water-lilies dead.
Moonlight salient on claws of the gate-rings –
this cool courtyard then empty halls then sky, white
dew-drops congealing on the wind,
emerald lacework heaped up on the terraces.
The dawn herald has gone, dawn is ablaze,
a raven on the gold well croaks, plane leaves fall.

Tenth Moon
Difficult to pour from the arrowlip jade cup.
The lamp smiles in petals, darkness frozen into light,
broken frost-strips diagonal on silk curtains.
> Her high room is lit by dragon-painted candles,
> under a pearl curtain she sleeps, moans, cannot sleep,
> under the gold phoenix dress she feels cold.
Eyebrows that surpass the crescent moon.

Eleventh Moon
The palace walls stretch into cold daylight,
a broken white sky sheds snowflakes.
> Bells! this wine has waited a thousand days,
> drink against the cold, drink to the Emperor!
Royal moats and fountains frozen in white rings.
Where are the wells of fire, the warm springs?

Twelfth Moon
A pale red glow from the feet of the sun,
some rime still under cinnamon boughs,
rare warm breezes contest the winter,
long nights ending, long days begin.

Intercalary Month
Emperors show their splendour
as years show their seasons:
72 days falling over each other
ashes flying from jade tubes
extending the year, so why
are we waiting?
Motherly time offers the emperor
the peaches of immortality while ministers
release their dogs into failure.

Airs at Furthest Accord

Listening to Fayrfax in Haute Provence October 2007

Beyondness growing from the small skin, small
oak trees spread across southern Europe
    Swallow, earthen dart, return
    air-broken, lashed to the crystal that
    turns round the earth We are locked
out of death until the message is delivered
and our progress settles, back into the moment's
wild spin. Can't you hear it unfolding from the palate
sweeping over the white rock of Europe
the cities that cower and inflate, doesn't the swift
wind on the crest call us out of hours doesn't
a far-fetched thought of calendrical pact
settle on the meadows after harvest? A call
    in the far fields and we turn as a returning
    swallow turns in parabolas among the roofs
and grazes the dog's head marking his
faithful progress on the dusty road,
locket at his throat for it is
in the end the true dog that trots
the length of the road bearing the account,
a European story or long song that the children will sing
at the turn of their days summing all the wrong
they have to own, all the knowledge
and shame of the proceeds. No one else bears it,
there are no substitutes for the dog, the dear
devoted dog who walks the road, the linear dog.
The thief doubles back behind the angel
the ministers of hatred divide the flame
the hills wrapped totally in small oaks
take a yellow edge towards the ending of the day
that pulls our hearts sideways into question
but only a steadfast mongrel passes by.
And presumably one day the dog's journey will end
with a pat on the head and a scratched ear, as we
cannot end, but sweeping a hand over Europe
as if to calm the world, pass into dream, the last
    spray of seeding flower-heads flung into the air.
And families broken and scattered

by war or paranoia travelling on the plains notice
a swallow returning with no message
but its own, the arrow of its being.
The dog has the message, and walks on
among trees, between people's legs on market day
up the street and over the hill and beyond.

The Road...

The road to Baghdad, is it level? Do they
kneel beside it to their own passions, ink-
wells of light, the rose that becomes a route?

Only the wounded pass through the gate showing
their red passports, only the killed arrive home
and take their mothers' coffee.

The stained floor of the desert, vultures wheeling
over the tank routes, forgotten tunes in the
far hills. Death steps over the river on stone syllables.

Sky full of stars, body parts flung out of transport systems
or suburban markets, dissolving into the greater
and closer light, moon on silent prophet's tomb.

Is this journey legal? Is it permitted? All that's left
of Palestine, a few small red flowers close
to the ground, a seething patience.

Kneel among them and beg for such patience
while the dove sings in the cedar, the song
of Yes, there will be pain, yes,

There will be horror at the dark traverse.
The coffee simmers on the heater,
its perfume fills the room.

The Road (remix)

How long, Babylon, how much more
blood soaking into sand, glitter-
ing safety on the floor?

A goat bleating under an olive tree
beside a ruined wall at the end
of a dry track, soldier,

This is the home you fought for,
grey stones tumbled on the ground
and a wooden flute serenading death.

The black eagle flies from cairn to cairn
with red messages: we shall make
our final space in sung words.

And in the vast green plains and hills of
eastern Europe the Jewish population
completely eradicated, not a stone on a stone

Not a board nailed to an upright. A wreath
of rose petals and bone for what remains.
Take it in patience, listen to the pain

In the dove's throat, water
pouring from the well, beating
of wings in the air.

The Road (carol)

To Bethlehem, is it really not very far? Do the shepherds
come to the road's edge to beg for dollars?
Do the hawks' star-shot eyes keep watch from above?
And when you get there, is there a hospital?

Cuban Nights

People dancing in ones and twos, catching the rhythm
through the back wall of the concert hall among
the evening rum vendors, nowhere else to go and poverty
again displays its gay plumage, elegant forgetting.

The dance is intellectual, the mind
balancing its routes, setting
paradigms of hope against lapse out of
sheer necessity, the leaf spinning from the tree.

The apotheosis of those who do badly,
sailing into city corners with one lamp burning.
If to do badly were the same
as to do harm, we'd know what to do.

But we live where we are and inhabit
our lives like a warm scent in the air pursued
through the streets towards guitar music and singing,
the voices edged with age, always saying goodbye.

And past forgetting is a social rightness remembered,
sitting in an old steel-frame chair in the yard
while the children run around and dance –
sunflowers, bean plants with small red flowers.

Dreaming in La Habana

Of the 'freedom of artists and intellectuals',
of the freedom to wreck everything
and reduce a society to a range of
aggressive sales pitches, and forget the promise.

The dogs bark all night, there is dancing
in the dark street under the street lamps to the rhythm
that escapes at the back of the concert hall,
with small glasses of rum.

The promise trembles on the edge of capitulation
to large-scale inequality for the sake of nothing we really
need. But a warm ease settles on the street at night,
a rhythm, an island pride. What remains of the state's duty?

Protect, distribute evenly and be incorruptible, the dream of nation.
Later the dancing stops and the rooftop cockerels prepare for their alarms.
Thin streets that know neither beggars nor homeless
slowly give access to small lines of light.

To the Memory of Frank Cassidy

I can't play properly now. Never could, really.
Slow subdued Irish speech and immediately
broke into a 'Bonnie Kate' that would raise every hair
of a bald man's head followed by 'The Blackbird' at which
the soul lies face down on the green slopes of earth
hoping for political good into the dawn

Which comes bright or failed, levers itself onto the hill
wrapped in thin rain and those of us who are blackbirds
will whistle and sing to it, and like all good workers
pass on to unmarked graves for the sake of the good
that goes unacknowledged and builds piecemeal a future
with enough cracks in it to evade political determination.

And I did nothing else, and everything I did
was done by these barren shores where the grey rock
breaks at the sea's edge, milled into the dawn.
It was the only thing I could do, the rest was shift,
and I did it all for Bonnie Kate, who was lost to us by politics,
but I followed her ship into a packet of gold leaf.

Weddings of the Gypsy Flower Sellers

The world image spins in the abandoned theatre (O nubile shade etc.)
birthday ribbons pulled through scissors 'Then somehow
my heart became a nightingale' opened its wings and flew
as blood flows, paths of haemoglobin through deserts of speech.

> *Devla, Devla*, what shall a poor gypsy do, but sing (not
> by Léhar) and tremble at the adversity heaped
> on a forked thing. O God who made me don't
> abandon me now but speak and I'll go.

> *Dela*, dance, so you can be seen, little taper
> give more light, little birch-wood taper.
> Ah *roma* we live well in night corners, our minds fly
> over the trees on beeswax wings 100 versts
> hour by hour *romale-le*, stealing big thoughts
> at night when nobody uses them.

> Where have you gone little gypsies *kaj jone romale*
> don't leave me now, for we shall live, not die
> and live well together. *Hey brother,*
> *have you seen any of our lot, with bears and monkeys?*
> Get into the car we'll find them.

The aesthetic supports the ethic and bears it further away
from God, who knows nothing and issues frantic edicts, forgetting
that He is the world and can't do anything but dance.

> *O Devla Devla*, what shall we do and where go, *cigányok*,
> to live somewhere, speak and wander (dance and sing)
> and hold the bright earth in its sky,
> empty theatre, resonant home.

This House...

This house on a Greek hillside with its geckoes and millipedes
wind bringing rain down from the mountains, the shutters
closed at night. Me with my mill-talk quieted, lying here
in the night and weather trying not to remember
failed claims pains of inarticulation and true attachments.
I don't forget. I don't remember very well.

There were never any gods of rain, peasant of the elements
who gets on with the allotted task and washes the white stones
on the red path, slides them down the hill. That rushing sound.
That particular brow. Unerasable intimacy. Far from here
northern town cold night wet streets curtains closed glow
of radiator red in dark room, illuminating the hangings.

Anywhere, a coming together and making a voice, a god's work,
a voice for ever, a voice at large, in the mountain sides
the small mills in stream clefts turning their wheels at night, that
rushing, hollow sound. A double voice of solitude and connection
melancholy and ecstasy writes itself into channels of the earth
as we dream between walls at night of distant points of contact.

This house on a Greek hillside with its geckoes and millipedes
and painted walls. The vast wars raging across the earth
the law of the heavier weapon... When the heroes come we run and hide,
we peasant faces, irrelevant elements, we are lost and done for
and kick stones in the road, the dirt road that winds up
into the hills. Our sighs run back down the meadow.

The god's eyes looking suddenly up to us in the carved stone,
the warm air wafted up from the heater, stirring a few cobwebs
on the ceiling rose. Two fires signalling across Europe. I'm
twisting my voice out of its body to rescue a glimmer of recognition
from the blasts of warfare. I'm working hard at this:
I'm not singing and not shouting. I'm looking for a stone.

All the pebbles I've picked up from the desolate shorelines of Europe,
a worn grey stone with a straight white line across it from Denmark
I press this stone into the world body, the dark mass,
to make there a small silence, in which we can hear each other
and the faint sounds the insects make, the grasses hissing in the wind
the unrepresented voices of the generations. In the hard edge

Of this sphere the dead also speak, massed seeds in flower heads,
and gain a recognition, participate in a chorus which strips
me of sad particulars, could I begin to address the issue,
by stones, yellow flowers, CD players, anything that works and say
that in the orkestra my guilt will modulate into the collective.
Well it may, or some other voice while the sun
sinks under the earth and we tune our voices to its echo.
Voices working together, for an honest peace, for sense
in the structure, for tangle threads that connect across the indigo.

The Lark in the Clear Air

Is. I've never known what to say.
But is and is. Calling over the / what's
that grass stuff called? I'm 70 this year
and something flutters in the sky that has
a meaning, and the meaning is
telegrams from the far edge
saying (and I shan't let go of this linkage)
that in order to live you have to die
which is banal but accurate and disguised
in song lifts the heart to a waltz with fate
which is not any old body's possession.
Good luck to you, new bird,
in the mean years to come.

Essex Skies

I

A failure, but it is the same for everyone in the end,
in the dark, under the lights. Driving back from
the wedding between the dark fields, the night layers
carefully hand aeroplanes down to Stansted,
and somewhere over the fields is a small embanked lake
with one elm, under which the controller
of weddings and stars sits crouched, tapping messages
to the enormous circular horizon. *Think what you're doing,*
the ultimate purpose of everything we do is to attain good.
And all that wealth in the sky, the sparkling
aeroplanes gliding down like swans to Stansted
to deliver cargoes of people back to their worries,
their weddings, their new babies. The dark field corners
are open to the great circle of mind, but waves of fear
shake the tree canopies. The earth turning brings
sky to the heart of its circle, across which
the indolent aeroplanes flashing and droning move
like waitresses from one side to the other of our
wedding feast, our immense resilience
and inevitable failure: big words
that shake the trees in the night, soundlessly,
black webs on black depth, interrupted by stars
and aeroplanes, following their rulers
and controllers, directing all that wealth
away from homes, into black holes.

II

The skies here are never less than total, and to live
under such spatial wealth must enclose you
in particulars: night fears, golf scores,
trouble with gypsies. The weddings call in
clans of hundreds, all offering their own fates
over which the principal celebrant is the baby, two weeks,
a superb performance and doesn't believe a word.
Career anecdotes, sex jokes, regulation and subsidy,
the baby has it all worked out and receives the applause
with graciousness. Nothing else unites this society.

And miles away, right out of earshot,
the travelling fortunes encircle a pivot, keeping
rigorously to flight paths coiling towards rest
and someone sits under the elm
in the dark beside the still water
singing *sotto voce*, controlling nothing
but her own heartbeat, inhabiting the rare
release of calm which unites this society.

Euston Road

Out into pouring rain. News vendors in red boxes. *They will cut off your head and run away with it so you cannot think* and cannot deploy the knowledge gained in courts of equity life-long. Never stop thinking: the dangers ahead, the inward turn of the market, what to do with an inadequate umbrella, run. To a subway. Emerge. Dive for a shop doorway. The dream on offer is birth, turning from death's clear portal. They lurk in red meat alcoves, shouting war, naming names. *The only names you need to know are those of the powers that obstruct a good fate.* Cower, at the rain, at the hard journey anticipated, into the Street of the Many Hotels, naming without meaning.

Argyle Street

World, world, we owe you nothing but you press us down. At least I have defeated the traffic scam. *There is a spell, world, against your weight, and the bright sparks that clog our feet.* I have forgotten this spell. Someone, world, stole my mouth and I shan't find it among the refurbished hotels, where shreds of hope are spun in the small hours. World with your gliomas and your bibles, damn you world. *May the fire burn you, bitter world, may the earth smother you.* This spell I learned in a field in Romania, probably it is obsolete. Sometimes the best response is to burst into tears, and see through the mist what we are. Not doing that, but something lesser, I turn into a hotel entrance to shelter from the deluge and complaints

Derbyshire House

of society. It is not a hotel, it is one of those blocks with a covered entrance. A man clutching a motorbike in the alcove, waiting for the rain to stop. He has nothing to say. He has a message to deliver. *Everything you see could suddenly disappear in a stroke of vengeance leaving dust and rubble and parts of people like red rags on the road.* Only a world concept can provoke that. The rain lessens, the messenger drives into it and I carry on down Argyle Street, out of the hotel zone into the council flats zone. I don't think I have the password for this but nobody's noticed me

Whidborne Street

yet. *You who heap plastic tricycles and defunct TVs on your balconies, respect my silence as I pass by in the rain.* I say nothing and I don't know your name, nor the tension in your living-room nor the fire behind the heart. Don't shake your enormous shorts at me I have the Book of the Dead in my pocket and I recognise the wallpapered grave. So far so good, the doors stay shut. *We are bound back to back, we never see each other, we never speak* turning the corner past the

Cromer Street

laundromat where a little old Asian man in a white robe runs through the rain head bowed, pink flower patterns on his shoulders. *Walk. Song. Thesis. Inscription. Make up your mind what you intend to be.* Passion's monument, older and deeper into solitude where people carry plastic bags in a hurry under cloud. A small split in the sky, a blue flag in the wind. I need a ferryman to take me across my eye, over to the east, the breaks of bright pastoral colours (sky, leaf) over ground stone. The boat is in pieces and I can't name the parts, the oars are words *They have reduced what is great to what is little. They have created war and internment.* The pedestrian lights change and the river stops to let me across. My eye

Judd Street

has a floater, I didn't need a ferry. And continue through the smallness, with the tall buildings on the right (on the way back they will be on the left) shadowing progress. The shadow in the desert, that enlarges the small traveller's longing for home. The air clings, the water runs along the sides of the roadway and down grids. This is a diagonal journey across a N–S grid, left right left right, go east go south bit by bit street by street until we arrive. The labyrinth has no centre but the true voice which is not so hard to find. The big building is a hostel. *They have created war...* What are their names? *I don't know their names. It was a long time ago and they are all dead.* It was yesterday and the widows are still shrieking. *My speech went down the grid* but I have reached the very heart of my pupil. Another right

Tavistock Place

turn, polished red brick of apartment block. It's a short street, but its name continues ahead, into death and destruction, like a spark at the end of the street, caught in the target, core of the retina, an ordinary morning. 'The senses report to the heart, which forms thought and sends it to the mouth. Opening the mouth re-enacts the conflict between Horus and Seth.' Walls polished by blood, body parts flying through the air. *Cut the hole for my mouth, I have something to say* we have brought war on ourselves, and daily fear, on the very edge of our enlightenment, which stands but a few yards SE of here: Coram Fields, Handel Street, Brunswick. Orphanage, health centre, public gardens. A global pact. But still the eye is drawn towards crisis, a flash and bang at the end of the street. We are blasted OUT. They are sucked IN. Avert the eye and turn another corner, to the left, avoid the crux or thought remains for ever unformed, numbed under blame. At

Marchmont Street

every corner I become a different creature: now I'm some kind of tall crocodile in the shopping zone. *Gods in caves, eating the dead.* The dead of Tavistock Square and the dead of seven wars. And who will believe us when we say there is nothing to fear from the distant villages on the edge of the desert? *Somebody has cut off my head and is eating it in a retail outlet.* Day and world bound together, back to back, eyes that never meet. To enter every shop in Marchmont Street one by one and buy back the body parts, for reassembly, to reconstruct a people out of their debts. And what is this people? *It is not me, it is not you, it is not Islam and it is not 'us'.* So hurry. And keep eating, eat as you walk, eat up the fear, words are food, grab a vocal sandwich and sing, consume and be consumed. Sooner or later the outcome has to be settled, war or peace, fragments or wholes, everlasting despair or vast hope free from distractions, resentment, impotent rage. There's plenty of time. Gather the parts together as you pass Brunswick Square, recently translated from shopping to corporate spectacle. *The creatures that live in the pupil of the eye* are called into assembly, and stand in a row looking at a glass-fronted housing development maturing into the sky. A city made for the people. The people here and the people there. Regency

Russell Square

clearances preserved for the commonalty while business interest scowls in concrete sheds round the back. A fountain at the centre, and unconditional welcome. Also a nasty report in the distance up

Woburn Place. Destruction of substandard dwellings, destruction of persons by random violence: a state, a world state, is at work, spreading its double wings. Where is the person that we need, *den Die Todeslust der Völkner aufhalt /* who restrains the death wish of the people? *Expect no heroes, no singularity. A patchwork of body parts.* There's some kind of hope just round the corner. *I have turned eight corners and passed through eight states as eight creatures* and now I am in an open space between night and day with a fountain at the centre. It's not far now, round the last corner. I shall arrive separately as each of nine mummified ibises to listen to the music of the eastern lute. It's starting to rain again. I asked a load of questions and they weren't answered. The music that approaches (round the corner) is the fall and rebirth of the city. It says, *I wish I were a swallow, then I could sit on the top of the Gherkin among the uncountable rods and watch the city centre squirming and fighting across its channels and struggling to make sense of its thousands of streets along which contradictory wishes crawl...* How to measure the pricing of our ease, and not link our fate to a dying oligarchy of oilmen. A bird with one wing dipped in blood and an illegible message written on the other beginning 'Within the bounds of hope...'

Round the corner and up the steps. Before me the island of the horizon dwellers, *the floodplain at harvest.* I hear the wing beats from the basement. The open mouth, the unlocked doors, of the shops, of earth and sky, the message rising from the peaceful centre of contemplation, a point without volume, free of hunger, a painted flower *'Within the boundary of the people' I eat the enemies.*

Western States (1)

—oOo—

1   Unsustainable light, discontinuous song, unpayable debt. A display of surplus energy not yet accounted for: a burning cauldron, a mass of bright lights surrounded by blackness as the plane descends towards Las Vegas. And before you've got your foot on the ground the music of it surrounds you: tinkling gambling machines – mesmerised, already. Hire a car and get out of it, past the towers of light, the shining monuments to credit – look in amazement but go on, into the night. The desert either side of the road pitch black, the desert of fun pitch bright disappearing behind to a flicker and we are alone. Such lights will always leave you alone, looking for somewhere to lay your head.

2   We go on and on, the black desert alongside, it gets later and later. We pull off at a motel sign: Glendale. A row of closed doors with bright light shed on them, an owl sailing over, machine noise in the night. The quietness of American confidence, always with machine noise in the background, for the running never stops. We can't stay here, we get back up onto the big road, the night-running road that brings the necessities from afar, for none of them grows here. Quiet road now, but not stopped. 100 miles from Las Vegas, perhaps we'll have to drive until dawn, but then there's an exit lane down to an outlying piece of funland rather unimaginatively called 'Oasis', open and not exactly busy, but at work. It's 3 o'clock. Evidently the fun never stops.

3   Wake to an American blackbird on the lawn among grey apartment blocks. This place costs so little, dispensing the easy, calculated generosity of the surplus: cheap accommodation, plentiful breakfast to the music of gambling machines on the floor below, protected from daylight, tended by Hispanic

and Asiatic servants, of course. Glimpses of bare sandy hills between the blocks. Plenty of room in the parking lot, plenty of water in the supermarket, plenty of everything in the desert.

4 A dirt trail departs from the interstate and leads to a fence round a couple of trailers on a rise of land in the desert, under the heat. At night a small cluster of electric lights, visible miles away. The resources of half the globe have been pressed into service to furnish these few lights in the desert, surrounded by broken stone. New housing developments on the flanks of desert ridges, walls round them, like fortresses. Who lives there, where are they from, what do they do, how will they manage with an unsustainable water supply and far too much light? What can you do with emptiness and excess all round you? Watch the TV, but every time you look up those elegant long-distance lorries cruising along the sandstone horizon.

5 We turn off the road and stand for a few minutes on this barren ground, red and brown, rock and grit in a long curve across to the distant ridges, dim in haze. A small rodent scurries away. Biblical landscape, as the Mormons recognised, searching for green pastures across vast nothing, that never changes and never has a thing to offer. But already the ironies are beginning to fade, and the desert to talk.

6 This would be where to sing the hymn that eludes me, to invoke the total in measured periods from a grave platform, like the tight shrubs with yellow flowers, all a regular distance apart. Such as the hymn called 'Africa': *God on his thirsty Sion-Hill / Some mercy-drops has thrown*. The world waits. *Deep on the palms of both my hands / I have engrav'd her name*. Africa waits, for the promise to be met, the metaphor to be untied. The desert mutters unintelligibly.

7 Springdale. All the old settlements are linear, follow the line of the valley and the thin thread of viability that runs down it. A few side tracks turning away between stony hills. In the motel a humming-bird tries to feed itself from the Stars and Stripes sticker on the glass doors. Unsustainable hope, we all know it very well.

8 Zion Canyon. Navajo sandstone towering above, monument to erased nations, seven chapters inscribed on the sides of the canyon in red ink, memoirs of the biggest emptiness of all. Neither the Pueblos nor the northern tribes could keep these places going: exhaustion of resources, outbreaks of war, under-nourishment, hysteria, all pack up and go. The eagle's eye stares down at the strip of running water far below bending this way and that and its green flanks, patches of grass and the tops of trees. Water stored in the

rock for hundreds or thousands of years, seeping out at the shale junction like sap, a whole river sustained by it. It runs down the river-side cliffs, spouts out of the canyon sides making green arbours and enclaves, waterfalls, dark pools with bats flitting over them, tree frog habitats. Mule deer browsing in the dark.

9   Nobody wanted it all that much. It had water but it didn't have width, extent of land. People were thinking of supporting future populations on the spot, not isolated smallholdings doing some trade. What population has actually thrived for any length of time here, or is likely to without massive external support? Zion area abandoned by Pueblo *circa* 1200.

10   A blue jay moves from one treetop to another. We are toiling up very steep tracks in extreme heat among masses of pale sandstone. Naughty chipmunks jump onto our backs. Great cliffs of white rock in strange tubular formations like elephants' legs. Dusty tracks across the pale tops among red bushes that dry into grey. The forms and conditions of the landscape are again biblical: the scarcity of resource, the water from rare clefts in the hills bringing precious sustenance in green shade, to sit under the tree and sing, the psalmic mode of earth-thanks for respite. Always at a frontier, searching for renewal, untrustworthiness of the newly gained ground. Experience then is forward, against a semi-nomadic shuttle service which follows the earth's results wherever they wander. It breaks out into multiple marriages and lonely deaths. The Indians also failed in this land, before the Spanish arrived, over and over again, but at least they failed unto themselves. Sadly triumphant American West, desert spreading over the world. Labor day in a drooping flag, bewildered.

11   Transcend this. Up on the highest zones, Carmel formation, white rock streaked red and pink in great flowing masses. Evening comes on, tidal winds develop, you hear them coming towards you as a hissing, brushing across the white rock while the light lowers. And the wind reaches you and breaks over you, then calm again. Then a new wind, white sound over white rock, coming across the tops, hardly stirring the tough shrubs that huddle in the lower clefts. Eventually the hills are lighter than the sky.

12   This would have been a good place to sing 'Abide with me', preferably in Joseph Funk's (1822) version, *parlando*, choral speech, if I could get together at least ten interested persons. Here, or a Mennonite wooden church in Virginia with the horse traps waiting outside and the whole of modernity given notice to quit. Under the whisper of the wind on the white rock, a fragile hope, a sustainable loss. And where after all is death's sting? It's on it's way, and still we smile, and offer a choral shuffle to the fall of the world.

13   Bighorn sheep near the car park, dimly visible in twilight, leaping over unsteppable rock slopes. Don't worry, Bighorns, the Sheepeater Indians won't get you now. Somebody got them.

14. We get back to the motel. Grand Teton Spring-grass India Pale Ale from the gas station and the quest for a bottle-opener. The nervous serenity of the non-combatant sometimes abides with us, busying ourselves elsewhere. Decision not to buy Polygamy Porter.

15   Evening and next morning both find us at The Mean Bean, a small unpretentious café on a side street. Cuba means poverty, and USA means wealth, but no Cuban would tolerate the quality of the blended coffee you are served everywhere here. Cubans expect the best. The only way to get a good cup is to find an independent coffee house, like The Mean Bean. Among books available there for browsing is a fairly recent demographic atlas of USA which shows the proportionate increase in 'non-white' populations clearly but also shows that even if they reach a sizeable majority they will not get power, because the 'white-only' states still greatly outnumber all others. It's not somebody's wicked scheme, it's the inherent structure of advantage, that it will perpetuate itself by enclosure.

16   Salt Lake. The wide-spread fertile valley with the flowing streams, the promised land, the earthly paradise, became a mountain of money as if that was its ultimate purpose, became a metaphor. Not much culture, but expensive uniform dark suits and a lot of eternity safely stored in the bank vault of the heart. But in the great nonconformist song books the happy land was essentially *far far away* and then we shared our portion with the rest of humanity.

17   A city founded on evangelism. Isn't that what America is all about? Joseph Smith, Ralph Waldo Emerson, Walt Whitman, Ezra Pound, Jackson Pollock. People getting visions, unable to see anything but what blinds them, getting the new dispensation and the world has to know, urgently. Striking the earth for attention, opening up pits and vaults.

18   But what was that hymn they sang? The enormous choir in the enormous concert hall vast as deserts disappearing into the distance. Is this the hymn that eluded me, with the trees of the river meadow moving behind it? 'Lead, kindly light' gently and firmly, with massive support: the sound of certainty, still touching even in its desertified form. The kindly light led us to the fruitful valley and the green pastures, and then into the bank vault and shut the door. Well, in song the enclosed always have the advantage, and we love them for it, bearers of the image of the ultimate home that they still long

for, now a metaphor. And we walk out into the open air, noting sadly that we shall never be able to lie with you in your monumental box. It is our loss entirely.

19   But, grateful for our existential anxiety we wander the town and successfully evade the recruitment drive, mainly by being away from the centre. It's good to be reminded by the Utah Folk Arts Museum that it is, or was, perfectly all right for big tough American farmers to pass their spare time doing elaborate crochet work, and we'll never get another farewell like the one we got from the lady in charge as we left: 'Thank you for your culture and your greatness.' I guess she was thinking of the country rather than us in particular.

20   And next day we drive over more mountains and find little to say about Bear Lake but it was great to be here and when do we expect to notice a recognisable native American? The bright blue, approaching turquoise, expanse and 'American rural' from there on to Jackson: timber-framed houses, centre-peaked wooden barns, wooden fences round corrals and quite moderate fields. Occasional small towns with false-fronted buildings. We have been here before, perhaps in France or in Romania or somewhere in Wales. Always mountains in the distance. We shall be here again. It's a kind of transcendental home, an idea of peace and production, very little to do with the actual people who live here, worthy as they may be. A kind of promised land always held in reserve in the mind, occasionally glimpsed in passing. A sentiment, but fairly well grounded in ecophenomenology (and so not an avoidance of politics) (but the very aim and purpose of politics). (My nervousness has drawn me into strings of parenthetical declaration again.) Most towns around here have false fronts; Jackson has false false fronts.

21   And shops which seem fairly normal or quaint outside and when you go in it fills the entire block. We have been here before, though the goods on offer didn't previously include a stuffed moose for $200,000. Is this a town or a theme-parked supermarket?

22   The sense of a town returns when you wander around in the late evening. There are signs. A row of old steel-framed chairs out in the street in a badly-lit space near the bus station with a few youths sitting on them. It could be Poland, or a fenland market town or the ledge round an Italian palazzo. They are not smoking the top brand Cuban cigars, tobacco 'grown from seed in Guatemala', that are on sale round the corner, and obviously the profits go somewhere else.

23   We sleep in a fake cabin, comfortably. Ranging through these contra-dictions is part of the adventure, glad to be here, holding a CD of mediaeval English carols by *Anonymous 4*, found in a thrift shop on the high street at $2. Working out how that could have got there will take up most of the night.

24   Sailing over Jackson's Hole and along the side of what accurate transla-tion can only call the Big Tit Mountains: a common enough mountain term (the Paps of Jura). And increasingly the land is spread out before us, where people don't live, as if they never did (though in fact they did). Not empty or natural but a product of human work, an excavation, a cleared space, a wildness factory.

25   An almost intact ecosystem, carefully nurtured. If one purpose of the polis is to facilitate the creation and maintenance of such things, then there is some sense in which the politics work and the common eye can see. Or at least, it makes no sense to say that Iraq had to be destroyed in order to run Yellowstone. That was to pay for something else, perhaps Las Vegas. Money is actually quite subdued in Yellowstone.

26   So through the pay station and enter, arriving just in time to see Old Faithful erupt, watched by about 200 people sitting on rows of benches, I thought for a moment they were going to applaud.

27   Vast stretches of forest, mountains, lakes, rivers plunging through canyons and winding through wide grasslands, people all over the place but dominated by the creatures, who move around about their business seeking fodder and prey and each other, in ('almost') their own terms. The rivers are fresh and strong and meander freely in great meadow and valley spaces, the canyons are deep and rugged, the forests seem to go on for ever. A construct of the earthly paradise, as sculpted to that image as any Renaissance garden.

28   Bison coming down to the river to drink in the morning. Bison wandering over the hillsides in scattered herds. Bison in the car park, standing looking at the cars. Bison head-butt each other, one of them picks a fight with a bicycle. In the herd the adult males keep up a steady low snorting rather like distant thunder, or bass snoring at close quarters. It's like a wall thrown round the community. Bison stroll down the middle of the road halting the traffic, brushing against the sides of cars. They have thick fur over their front half like a shawl, and the rear half covered only in tight black hair – like a ballet-dancer in a big tunic with padded shoulders and tights. A bison finds a dust patch and rolls in it, creating a cloud like a small geyser eruption. And from time to time there's a lone male bison ambling over the plains, one of those that lost the fight and didn't get himself a herd of wives and children, convinced Darwinians that they all are. The bison's

head: constant slow alertness modelled into a slightly capricious (goatish) mask through which peers the eyes' constant search for continuance.

29 Lone animals going about their businesses. A coyote walking over the meadows, stops and suddenly rises a foot in the air to descend on some rodent. A big moose wading in the edge of the river as if it has a long way to go. Is it a happy moose or a sad moose or is it just posing for the cameras? Who can tell? Is it saying to us, 'Here we have it our way' as they ('almost') do? 'We're willing to put up with you as long as you don't get in the way.' If we could manage not to get in our own way we might learn something about the earthly paradise.

30 The earthly paradise is in fact somewhat complicated by being situated over a hot spot, magma much closer to the surface than is either usual or safe. A caldera, a collapsed volcano about 50km across causing all kinds of disturbance. At the far side of the grasslands before the forest edge, puffs and shoots of steam going up, like a distant prospect of a busy railway station in the 1940s. In the mornings you notice that some of the rivers are giving off steam and clouds of it are projected into the air from roadside vents and springs. Not much of pastoral beauty when you enter the geyser basins, mostly an industrial aspect, the ground covered in various kinds of silicon effluent like the run-off from a chemical factory: browns, reds, yellows, blues, acid greens and white, while these things huff and puff and slobber through holes in the ground. Pools of boiling mud, ponds of bubbling water overflowing onto a hillside stripped of all vegetation. Plenty of colour but outstandingly barren, destroyed. Fumaroles, mud-pots, hot springs, many of them stinking of hydrogen sulphide. Extremophile microbes living on the boiling hot edges of the vents, cunningly using hydrogen as an energy source and adding to the coloration. And here and there a true geyser which will from time to time throw a great column of boiling water into the air, glittering in the sunlight. And the ground sizzles and bubbles and seethes with an energy which is a risk of the earth's entire structure.

31 One of these boiling amphitheatres would have been a good place to sing, with orchestral accompaniment, 'God save America', preferably next to an erupting geyser with umbrellas up. From its oil industry for one.

32 And unexpectedly, in a rather dark alcove in a shop selling plastic chipmunks, the remarkable Yellowstone watercolours of Thomas Moran, 1871-2. Paper stained by earth forms, amazement in the very brush-stroke. There is also a persistent tension in the pictures that bespeaks some anxiety, some dismay before these manifestations of the earth at its most capricious. There is some kind of backing off.

33   This construct of the earthly paradise retains an edge of fear. You can walk freely in the vast and open landscape, with the faint possibility of encountering at the worst a bear or a wolf, or getting the wrong side of a bison or elk, a fear which, especially as a newcomer, you can never relinquish, that edge is always there wherever you go. And the officially 'remote' possibility of the Yellowstone volcano going up again, last time was 600,000 years ago: the whole caldera, shooting several thousand cubic kilometres of molten rock into the air and destroying a large portion of USA, directly or by burying it in ash. Which portion depends which way the wind blows and Hispanics are traditionally very unlucky in these matters. It would anyway be the end of the state and no victim population to hold responsible for it. Lesser but devastating earthquakes are also available, the last 1975. These things 'never happen'. We could cultivate our fear as a kind of lens, we could get out of the habit of assuming that only sections of Africa and Asia are doomed parts of the world.

34   To think you can eradicate anxiety. Build such defences round an enclave of heavy profit-takers that nothing can ever touch it, neither want nor accident, not the poor or the blacks or the whole of the Southern world. Destroy any country whose resources you need including your own. And nobody will fight back, you can fix that, no trouble, they will fight each other. But insecurity is our birthright, we can't act without it. It keeps us upright. It keeps us out of trouble. It keeps us alert to the world's tricks. Without our fear, which includes concern, we are imbeciles. And the false fears gather round us in the night.

35   In the forest camping ground at the end of the day, squatted round, heating cans of meat and bean mixes on a wood fire in an iron ring. A few bottles of Spring-grass Ale still left, rather warm. Soon to sleep, or try to, on hard ground with cold feet, worrying what a bear's tread would sound like. What imbeciles!

36   A charmed zone but it has no fences round it. Bears and ghosts move freely in and out of it, ghosts of Indians, miners, dead antelope, that pursue you through the Rockies. We are on the road again, through a zone of serious destruction by earthquake (1959) and another of serious destruction by theme-parking and a lot of up and down and on and on passing several fairly tired looking settlements, the occasional herd of pronghorn, and a lot more trees, and by mid afternoon up Big Hole Valley following a school bus that stops to drop its charges every few kilometres at ranch entrances or the ends of tracks. Then a lesser road to the south and then another, further into the side of the valley, and roll slowly along a dirt track to a ghost town. O could the entire USA power but fix itself into 'arrested decay'!

37   Bannack. Late enough by the time we leave to be on the edge of evening. No other visitors left, the woman in the shop beginning to pack up. Another two hours and the place will have separated itself from its history. Evening, with its blues and browns, and a street of empty wooden houses stands as no more than what it is, as things do at closure, in a state of 'arrested decay'. A bob-tailed rabbit lopes around in the quietness, evening wind coming down from the hills slightly moves the grass in the spaces between the houses, and behind the houses, among the outbuildings, the space with the bar where the horses were hitched, the wide grassy high street. A dimness starts to gather on the further spaces beyond the town, the cemetery on a hilltop, the gallows below it, the wrecked watercourses where the gold was dredged up, bits of derelict machinery hanging in shreds from the bank. The gold lies there, inert, diffused in the ground on which the two rows of houses stand, the light wind brushing between them. All the violence and desperation stilled: in the saloon with bullet-holes in the walls, in the church, in the schoolroom and the courtroom, in the family houses, in the small shacks further back where the bachelors and the whores lived, all the desire, for gain, for consummation, wafted away.

38   Likewise deep in snow in the winter. Likewise standing here, the day's last visitor, thinking that nobody ever sought anything much in this place beyond their own advancement, and would happily destroy anything that stood in its way, such as Indians and bison. Such as each other. There would surely be a resistance to that in the structure of settlement, wives and children would also claim their places and have their voices, with a right to be free of stray bullets, for the weather was already a hard enough master. If the town were to have any viability it was not going to be a crisis centre or cowboy film. I don't believe it was. The bench set at an angle of the outer wall of the house, facing into the street, small tree hanging over it: this place also had evenings. In which it disengaged itself from its history and from the fermenting energies of buried gold, the angry fear that projected it to this edge. Gunfire from the saloon, or a baseball hit gone amiss? (Yes, there was a baseball team.) The Indians too killed each other and wrecked their own strategies for survival in a difficult terrain (and played something not unlike baseball). Possibly they had something else, which didn't counter the harm so much as overrode it, or overrode prosperity itself, at a cost. Deep in the snow in the winter, they spent precious energy in dances aimed at reconciliation with the earth.

39   All the voices of the town's history merge together and disappear into the sound of an evening wind down the hill, and the mind dances in the wind in its own space. That faint brushing, cancelling sound is the only ghost. The 'communities': miners, farmers, Mormons, Indians, Hispanics, blacks,

80

Pueblos, ranchers... disappear into a common humanity which speaks a language of pre-thought through individuals at rest, through the colouring of their voices against the evening, the change a small sycamore makes to the sound of the wind. Follow that sound. Follow it along Route 278, fields so vast you think they don't have fields around here, containing thousands of Black Angus cattle. And come to a place called Wisdom (Montana).

40 Not much of a place, Wisdom. A gas station with appendages at a road junction. Two motels, two eating places, some houses somewhere. You don't need to seek out the special places, nor the worst; the extremes are by definition marginal. You can be where you happen to land. Ed Dorn scoured Nevada and Idaho looking for victims of power, seeking out the most impoverished Indians in the worst reservations (but missed the 'miserable' Goshute) looking for some trace of spirit in a dying eye, some crisis anger on desolate islands. He would never be contented with what was lying around on the surface, he had to mine for it. What he extracted were the broken crystals of his own spirit, shattered reflexive surfaces, frontier development ending in a trance dance. It was a rodeo act at heart, the lustful quest for exhaustion. What does lie around on the surface of the land is what anyone can locate, the virtues that persist in the unexceptional. Such as to be remarkably cheerful in a one-horse town, like the one-armed man running the post office or the charming young waitress in the Big Hole Restaurant explaining the texture of Rocky Mountain oysters... There are faceted mirrors in people's speech and eyes that stir up our hope, and set us forward for the road. Isn't this spirit an achievement against the odds everyone faces, confronting the deprivation everyone faces, accelerated decay? We ask her if it's a good idea to go to the Antlers Saloon along the street. Yea why not, she says, meet the whole town in there. The kitchen staff want to know what I think of the oysters.

41 In the Antlers Saloon five men (there must be more to Wisdom than this) who start talking to you before your foot's over the threshold. Hi there, who are you, come and sit down here, how you doing? Perhaps this is the longed-for culmination of 150 successive evenings in the Antlers Saloon Wisdom with the same five men and one barmaid and suddenly *strangers* walk in, and a *family* and on top of all that, *British*! No problem, totally cool. It's as if a British family walks in here once or twice most weeks. That's some kind of achievement too.

42 People live here as they live anywhere, making the best, worst, or muddle out of it, until forcibly prevented by war or paranoia. The national increasingly seems like some kind of alien presence in these spaces, an intrusion of vacuity demanding to be filled, and minds are drawn into it as if it might be

a necessary completion of their being, while really it is nothing to do with them and creates unanswerable gaps in sense which can only be concealed behind false fronts, doors which won't open and there is nothing behind them. Like the lights of Las Vegas in the desert, while the desert is so much richer and brighter than the lights. And the rich and the powerful, what do they have to do with all this, and anyway, where are they? Everywhere we go they seem not to be around, though their beams are felt. They might be some form of extra-terrestrial. In UK there's no avoiding them, and their apes.

43   We sit in a row of three at the bar with amber ale. Kathy and Beryl get to talk to two men, a rancher and a telephone engineer, the ones who welcomed us in. They are calm and convivial, they seem like people who have given thought. I, as tends to be my fate, get the village drunk, who as drunks go is sympathetic and intermittently coherent. The official fear is upon all of them, but doesn't always show itself. At present what they are afraid of is Islamic terrorists and this will affect some of their actions, though their chances of coming across one are not great. They are not afraid of the sleeping volcanic caldera fifty miles to the east, with its bubbling mud pools and steam vents and fountains of boiling water, which when it finally erupts will probably destroy the entire North American continent. Should they be?

44   The drunk describes five kinds of fencing he knows how to construct, talks of blowing into a horse's nostrils, and then waxes poetical concerning the wide fields of Montana: 'I have a sky over my head as beautiful as the ceiling of the Sistine Chapel, I have a wonderful multicoloured carpet under my feet in spring, a rich brown carpet in autumn, a thick white carpet in winter…' The cool and serious men say Bush makes them feel ashamed to be Republicans. But the main condition is local: people talking to people in a saloon in a small town up in the hills of Montana, enlivening the day's ending and hopefully learning slowly, us too, to resist the fear of difference as best we can. Clear skies veiled in smoke from distant forest fires. In the morning there is ice on the roof of the car. The place still works. Wisdom works for breakfast, giant egg and bacon rolls and mugs of blended coffee. Wisdom works for petrol. Then forest and mountain without end. What you can't see is what you don't need to know.

45   You need to know about Big Hole Battlefield but you don't need to see it. And all the other battlefields, where the losers lost their persistent optimism and the big boys grew bitter at their success. You need to drive up valleys and over mountains and through more forest than you ever thought existed on the earth, and arrive at a city.

46   We shelter from the land for a while in company and professionalism, and the solid things that are possible in a working town, the operative peace recuperable at the centre of the American whirl. Racoons in the trees at night, liberal dissemination of knowledge and wonderful second-hand book and CD shops such as Britain decided, apparently, it didn't need. The smoke of distant forest fires moves over the town, a momentary storm blows pieces of wood down the street and the edges press in. Here we bought the song about the killing floor. Eyeing the unforgettable, unforgivable edge that never leaves us, we take it easy in the liberal theatre entitled to its own space. Very good Californian pinot by Rodney Strong and a delicious Mexican shrimp soup.

47   South-west from Boise, over the Nevada border and due south. 'The loneliest road in America' – not this one, but one that crosses it at Great Basin and reaches California, but this is a good second. Highway 93, Twin Falls to Las Vegas, 476 miles, 50 miles or more between most settlements and some of them so small you don't notice. Nevada, dumping ground for Indian tribes surplus to requirements and nuclear waste. Jackpot, Contact, Wells, Currie… Semi-desert emptiness, pale stony ground, sagebrush stretching away in all directions, grey shrubs and patches of grey grass, always mountains in the far distance. Every now and then a dirt track goes off and disappears towards the far mountains, trailing away out of sight, and ending where? A shack in the edge of the hills with just about enough water and land to support a dedicated loner? A ghost town, derelict mine, hunters' lodge, hippie camp, or the track just stops somewhere among the scrub, trailing into nothing? 'Snow Water Lake' beside the road, two or three miles of salt crust.

48   We stop at Goshute Station which was a roadside store and bar before it closed, and is now an abandoned retail outlet in the desert with, behind it, a scatter of white huts in which, it is difficult to believe, people must live. I could imagine it as a kind of Taoist retreat, empty mind on vacant ground. An elderly woman comes out of her door to examine the post box, finds nothing and goes back in, surrounded by sky and earth. Having so much distance all round you, what difference does that make? If you don't (and we, being English, don't) take it for granted, are you not both very small and enormous at all times? As you breathe in and out? Inhaling the scent of Great Basin sagebrush, low grey bushes with yellow flowers, stretching into a distance nobody can do anything with.

49   You can see a great deal further than is normal, but the further you see the shorter you see and you can't see the social or the national at all. The social is elsewhere. The national is absolutely extra-terrestrial and is using your enormous garden as a rubbish tip.

50   Nuclear waste dumps, military training grounds, bombing and gunnery ranges, prisons, vast fields of silence where aliens picnic. And over there beyond the hills to the east are the Goshute reservations, in one of which the Indians were, last I heard, campaigning to be allowed to have the USA's biggest spent rods dump sited on their land, for the sake of the rental, and representing the massive opposition to this from environmental groups and Utah State Council as yet further examples of the white man's assumption of the right to intervene in Indian affairs. 'Miserable' indeed.

51   And some loon in an unmarked car trails us at 100mph for 50 miles for reasons best known to himself until we gain refuge in Pioche, which is packed out because it's Labor Day, and there's nowhere to stay so we sit on the edge of the sidewalk in the dark to watch a procession of floats slowly descending the main street of the town. In comparison with this display the annual Sunday school walk in a suburb of Stockport in the early 1950s was a triumph of professionalism. Indeed some of them don't even manage to have lights and so can hardly be seen at all. The desert behind the houses is so much bigger than any of it and means something beyond accidence and risk. The edge expands into a diagram of long-term result. Somehow it is next morning, more blended coffee and we are on the road again, nervous but determined.

52   We stop at Cathedral Gorge Park. We walk into the desert, step a few metres off the designated path (though you are asked not to) and look down at the ground. Buff, pale sand, toned by scatters of grey stones and small tufts of hard grass, occasional blue-grey bushes without leaves. Indian rice-grass, rabbitbrush. The same here before your feet as over the far side of the valley. Bentonite clay. Temperature 85F. Small low sand humps showing marks of lizards' and birds' feet and sometimes the streak of a tail. Delicate engravings on barely compacted ground. A record of millennia of weather and yesterday's news. Distant memory of a lake bed. Erosion, freezing and thawing, water running over the ground and disappearing, evaporating, dust gravel and sand in patches, different shades of buff. How full the mind becomes, standing in emptiness as a monument to itself.

53   Like the sudden copse of Joshua trees the other side of Caliente – suddenly something completely different, shocked by its context into concentration, among all that space and paleness a dark green pillar of sharp fibres, twisting at the top as if searching or commanding the sky. And 'needs a winter freeze before it will bloom'. Zen-like thoughts of perseverance as we reach the outskirts of Las Vegas. And notice as we approach that display of expendable wealth how very many people there are living in the concrete apertures under the roads.

54   Las Vegas only really exists from a distance. A cluster of electric fire in the black vacuity. When you get into it it's just a shoddy fairground with water conservation problems. The new architecture proves fussy and over-decorated, the black pyramid has a vodka advertisement plastered all over one of its faces; perhaps Egypt will successfully claim copyright. The big displays are plastic, fibreglass, they might even be papier mâché. 'Venice' is less than a postcard, it's stuck onto the first floor of a hotel in odd corners and has no detail. Treasure Island, nobody knows who wrote it. Hispanics handing out prostitute tickets. This, I suppose, is what they would turn Havana into if they could get their hands on it.

55   Slot machines. I once drove myself to despair with a slot machine arcade, in Prestatyn in 1952. There was a big wooden hut full of them, they took pennies and were mostly the kind where you flick a ball-bearing up into a vertical curve and it then tumbles down through a mesh of pins to enter or miss slots which pay pennies back. Mine missed. All of them. I went to beg for some more. They too missed. I got a third supply and they all missed. I was twelve and close to tears. Since then they have taught slot machines to sing.

56   All the halls of gambling machines, which are everywhere in casinos, hotels, airport lounge, stores, restaurants, are full of a musical chiming, a mingled audible sweetness, sounding very much as if it should 'give delight and hurt not'. It is because the machines all the time they are being used give out chimes to accompany their actions, and they are all tuned to the same scale. So there is this sweet ringing heterophony, this tintinnabulation, filling the air, which must represent the gambler's dream, and the dream becomes a presence, the edge folded in, and you enter it, and perhaps you live the dream even as you lose the cash, like the new shopping in general.

57   The exit from such a country could not possibly be simple. Echoes and concealments lie all over it. Delays, unhelpful (underpaid) staff, tricks of the trade, local corruption, and we find ourselves at a Quality Inn in New Jersey clutching US Airways food vouchers an hour after they stopped serving food. Television night. Call out for pizzas. Do we want 'Buffalo cutlets' with them? Next morning a black evangelical convention of some kind getting its breakfast, a dark-suited slow-moving satisfaction reminiscent of the Salt Lake Mormons. Mugs of blended coffee again, then a mini-bus trajectory across miles of depot land… *Good Morning America, how are ya?* Well and ill and overweight and in a dream.

58   Thomas Moran reappears in Philadelphia as Turneresque, with a Venice scene, architectural details metaphorised into a staining of light,

which he then brought to Yellowstone: landforms imprinting the surface of paper, with bleeding edges.

59   Long time travelling. Motels and diners, a different country with the same chains. Grab it quick before it dies of unsustainability. A day in an unknown city shooting up unanswerable questions. What happened to Quakerism when it crossed the Atlantic? Washington keeping slaves in his household while drafting the rights of man (unsustainability). How are you meant to handle plastic lunch holders? And there was something wrong with those buffalo cutlets with the pizza last night over and above the fact that it was actually chicken – urgent need for a supply of 'rest rooms' as these evidently delicate and bashful people choose to call them. But surrounded all the time by soaring early brick buildings like abstracted peaks, speaking of a sense of hope, a confidence which the nation gave you, or at least some of you, and the lost hope of all those who are not allowed to become Americans, which illumines the fragmented particulars. A glimpse at the end, and we turn our backs and head home. Under the circumstances it seems best to end with a paragraph struggling to be born.

Western States (2)

Western States (2) *was arrived at by glossing the 59 paragraphs of the travelogue* Western States (1) *to produce 59 small poems. The idea was to set the reportage structure of (1) completely into reverse, until the places exist only for the purpose of supplying imagery for the poems. Anyone who reads the two works in tandem should be aware that there are anomalies. The 17th paragraph, for instance, wasn't used and poems 17 and 18 both derive from the 18th.*

—oOo—

1

Unsustainable light flickering behind
the song cut through distance

shines, black and alone, o shine
for ever, black and alone.

2

Night road black desert
closed doors, never stop

never never stop
the machine that brings takes.

3

It's true what the blackbird whistled:
have it or do without

surplus wealth,
bare and barren hills.

4

Fortress housing, desert lights over broken stone
look around turn around switch it off.

5

Distant ridges dim in haze, stone under foot, red
and grey the book of emptiness, the final prize.

6

The hymn is the prize, and we'll all sing it
right here in sub-Saharan patience.

7

The working line, the stream
threading the valley we shall

never settle the difference, the
fond seeking that never finds

never will, but one trust
one bright thread, sung this side.

8

Red ink on the sides of the canyon, Navajo script
and the great emptying, the great advance.

9

We turn our backs and the deer
come to drink in the dark.

10

Zion, the red bushes age into grey
the frontier men into lonely deaths.

11

The wind that comes hissing over the white rock
of Carmel, the white friars

begging in the desert
lighter than the air.

12

The wind on the white rock whispering
'abide with me'

which we do and smile
as the world falls into green sockets.

13

Ye silly sheep a whole catering industry
died out in the desert.

14

End of a hot day spring grass India pale ale
decision not to combat American gas station night.

15

O mean bean, the advantage
perpetuates itself without anybody lifting a finger.

16

Far away as it all still is, the land
the people the shared portion.

17

Kindly light leading into darkness
dark happiness dark hope very loud music.

18

Knowing better than anyone
is our loss entirely.

19

Our culture, our greatness, our pride
elaborate anxious extant, doing our best with the needles.

20

Sustainable space, the land
in its distance, its work

shall we waste it in passing or dress it
in parenthetical sentiment, frozen raspberry cream.

21

If the town is a false town
if the price is too high.

22

The consequences sit in a row waiting for the bus
the profits drove elsewhere.

23

Where true night comes down on the false cabin
and I grow too old to dream an old round dance

somehow makes it across the Atlantic
and gets into bed, proudly anonymous.

24

Up there ice wedges, wild questions
down here peanut butter, smiling angels

asleep in the ornamental cabin
snoring the earth's answer.

25

Home across distance, the contradictions fade
and it is not for us, this physical earth.

26

So but if only here then *whoosh* be
faithful if you can.

27

The paradise of creatures, the fruit, the meadow,
the river, the blood flowing past us

our blood, nourishing the fir trees
our science locked in the garden.

28

Monumental creatures slow
and faithful as we likewise

though lost a moment stood and
flickered on the earth.

29

Loneliness of monuments and rolling stones
meeting of earthly eyes.

30

Extremophile poets inhale hydrogen
and stain the ground with others' blood.

31

God save us all with trumpets and umbrellas
and the earth abusing itself in the background.

32

Urgent messages in earth tones
blur into the fibres of the paper

geology turned inside out, anxiety
about edges, be they healed or sealed.

33

And what we see through the lens of our fear,
the way the wind blows, the bad luck, the cauldron dance.

34

Worried blues do keep us on the ground
shakes a bit poetical fright sorry flight.

35

Fire on the ground beans bubbling in the can
the car waits pale in the night like a hungry bear.

36

Ghosts pass through all the fences in the land
in search of the vanished tribes

the school bus stops at the start of a trail
a young boy with a rucksack walks into the land.

37

To walk out of the house and never return
leaving the door open leaving

a cup on the table my breath
on the mirror my name on the air

full of blue and brown evenings
and graves of the powerful.

38

Flecks of gold buried beneath the houses
African poverty under the stars.

39

Slow evening wind comes down the hill
the community disappears into

the sound of a small sycamore
that chases us to wisdom.

40

The last star on the black island
cutting into the poet's back on the way home

thorn mirror to the far mountains
their accelerated privatisation.

41

The unexceptional gains the threshold
come on in and sit down, stranger.

42

Meeting of minds
flowers in the desert.

43

Sometimes I live in the country sometimes
I live in the town sometimes

I take a great notion to engineer
a telephone and give thought that lies sleeping.

44

The words that resist the fear
hover in the air like star signals

ice crystals on the roof of the car let it
shine on me.

45

And they all died, at each link
I called his name.

46

Sometimes I live in the killing floor
sometimes I live in abeyance

where there's a good second-hand bookshop
there is hope for this machine.

47
The end of the road in a scatter of grey bushes
mind beginning something

out of nothing in nowhere, turning
towards life, pale stony ground.

48
Empty mind turns looks
around sees the real

'land without people'
and fills with bitterness

low grey bushes with yellow flowers
breathe in and breathe out.

49
To see so far and see nothing in the distance
the rubbish-tip you thought was called life.

50
Vast fields of silence
in the distance the sound of distance

miserable assumptions
prisons and nuclear waste.

51
To be lost in the dark
sitting on the edge of the sidewalk the vast

desert behind the houses draining everything of meaning
but the noun to be.

52

Small low sand humps showing
marks of lizards' and birds' feet

and sometimes the streak of a tail, delicate
engravings on barely compacted ground.

53

The mind completely distinct, dark and sharp edged
turns to command the desert sky

where concrete apertures
shelter the new tribes.

54

How long, Las Vegas, electric fire blazing
Havana at night, shadow city, how long?

55

I sing my bad luck and
all my life of bad machines.

56

Sweet chiming bells invite us to
perpetual Christmas milking.

57

People in a dream, clutching
a ticket, a voucher

must get chicken fat run around we
ain't got long to stay here.

58

Something spreading in the grained surface
knowing we don't have long

stains the light
and unbinds the appetite.

59
Long ways from home a permanent
sense of hope illumines the particulars

the brick towers and the plastic lunch boxes
struggling to be born

I'm going back where I come from
good old dog, we never lost hope did we.

Notes

The Glacial Stairway

Words in foreign languages not translated in-text:

Part One

p. 7   *un mundo mejor es posible*
       a better world is possible

p. 9   *Baudelaire: ...en parfaite paix avec moi-même...*
       ...in perfect peace with myself and the universe, in my perfect beat-
       itude and total forgetting of terrestrial evil, I even came to think not
       so ridiculous those who claim that humankind is born good... [*hiatus*]
       ... and a piece of cake is enough to start a war.

p. 9   *Je suis le veilleur du Pont-au-Change / du Point de Jour*
       I am the watchman of the Exchange Bridge / of Daybreak

p. 9   *Luchar contra lo imposible y vencer!*
       Struggle against the impossible and win!

Part Two

p. 17 *media vita*
       in the midst of life [we are in death]

p. 18 *Sonos eternos jóvenes rebeldes!*
       We are young rebels for ever!

p. 19 *Ospita* is a word I invented as title to a poem sequence which can be
       found in *Passing Measures* (Carcanet 2000). It stands for some kind
       of healing structure, or the will to one.

Quoted from substantially or leaned on heavily:

Baudelaire, 'Le Gâteau' (*Le Spleen de Paris*)
M. J-F. Bladé, *Études géographiques sur la vallée d'Andorre*. 1875
Robert Desnos, 'Le veilleur du Pont-au-Change'
W.G. Hill, *The Andorra Report: an undiscovered fiscal paradise*. 1991
Robert Juarroz, *Vertical Poetry*, translated by W.S. Merwin. 1988
D.H. Lawrence, 'Bavarian Gentians' (the quotation near the start of Part
    Two)
David Lewis-Williams, *The Mind in the Cave*. 2002
Michel Maffrand, d'après A. de Musset, 'Le cançon de Barbarine', sung by
    the group Balaguèra.
Iris Murdoch, 'Thinking and Language'. 1951
Peter Riley, *The Linear Journal*. 1973

Robert Roberts, *The Classic Slum*. 1971
Troubadors: mainly Raimbaut d'Orange
Three songs from Calabria in Italian and Italianised Greek performed by the
group Nistanimèra
Slogans (in Spanish) on walls in Baracoa (Cuba) and on billboards in Havana,
noted in March 2006

See also: Peter Riley, 'Alpine Zones: the reward', in *The Day's Final Balance:
uncollected writings 1965–2006* (Shearsman 2007), pp. 192–5.

Best at Night Alone

pp. 34, 37 'Street, street, banal / baleful street…' – *Utca, utca, bánat utca…*
Hungarian song.

p. 36 'Lord God, you who made me…' – *Fă-mă, Doamne, ce mi-i face, Fa
mă-un gruz mare de sare…* Romanian song.

p. 39 'The wine sings in the bottle'. Baudelaire did indeed write this, as
quoted by John James, who saw it emblazoned on the end wall of a
coopératif in Languedoc.

p. 40 Caterpillars: Fabre's most famous experiment consisted of capturing
a band of processionary caterpillars, who every morning emerge from
the ground and process up a tree trunk to the leaves in a long line,
and placing them round the rim of a large urn in a continuous ring.
Contrary to the belief that they had a natural leader, he observed that
in that situation they continued marching until they died of exhaus-
tion. Each caterpillar had no urge other than to follow the back-end
of the one in front of it, and the 'leader' was in fact lost.

p. 43 'Fifteen Ekelöf Incipits': this page originally consisted of a list of
fifteen opening lines by the Swedish poet Gunnar Ekelöf
(1907–1968), in Swedish or English, all beginning with the title words
of this sequence, 'Best at night alone…', or some other formulation
of the same condition. Unfortunately it has not been possible to quote
these lines.

The Road…

The first three lines of 'The Road…' are adapted translations of four phrases
from the poems on pages 111 and 112 of Adonis, *Le Livre* (al-Kitâb) traduit
de l'arabe de Houria Abdelouahed (Seuil 2007).